The Kingdom of Scent

Enjoyable activities using your dog's natural instincts

Anne Lill Kvam

Published by
Sheila Harper Ltd.
2008

Photographs by Anne Lill Kvam, Gerd Köhler, Silvia Föller,
Sheila Harper and Bjørn-Owe Holmberg
Diagrams by Marian Tague
Picture/diagram captions by Sheila Harper

Written in English by Anne Lill Kvam
Edited by Sheila Harper, Connie Harper, Jean Gough and Carol Northcott

First published in Norway in 2005
Title of the original Norwegian version:
Nesearbeid For Hund ISBN 82529-2926-6
© 2005, Anne Lill Kvam

UK version published by
Sheila Harper Ltd
9 The Meadows
Rugeley
Staffordshire WS15 1JH
England.

www.sheilaharper.co.uk

Registered in England no: 6069259

Printed by
The Benhill Press Ltd.
Brook Square
Rugeley
Staffordshire WS15 2DU
England

ISBN no: 978-0-9548032-2-3

The Kingdom of Scent
Contents

Foreword

Having worked together with Anne Lill Kvam over the last ten years, I have realised just how much passion she has for her work. Precise, innovative and creative, Anne Lill knows how to develop a superb working relationship between owner and dog. She is one of the few who can truly apply theory to practical work, but her work goes further than this: Anne Lill also understands body language and takes into account how dogs feel. This in itself gives her a distinct advantage over other trainers, and means that she can achieve results with dogs that other professionals would be hard-pressed to emulate.

Anne Lill has a special gift, one which she is determined to pass on to others, and one which makes working with dogs much more accessible. I urge anyone wishing to build a relationship with their dog to follow her lead and take the first step towards a mutual understanding by entering the Kingdom of Scent.

Sheila Harper

Some of the dogs who have taught me so much about the Kingdom of Scent

Jane in Angola,
playing with the top of a landmine

Ynnie, a mine detection dog I worked with in Angola. I couldn't leave her behind so she spent her retirement with me in Norway

Troll, my standard Poodle

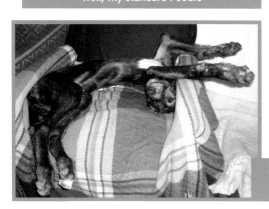

Glenshee, my Scottish Deer hound.
Exhausted after tracking!

Troll, in snow

Anne Lill Kvam and Chico

Preface

This book has become a reality as a result of giving courses around the world for a number of years. I teach simple ways of doing nose work with dogs: mainly tracking and scent discrimination. The students range from pet owners to professional dog trainers and search and rescue people. Almost everywhere I speak, students ask if I have written a book yet...
Now I have.

In all aspects of my work with dogs, the real thread is a passion for them both as a species and as individuals, along with a respect for their needs, their natural language and their behaviour.

When we humans are involved in training dogs for a few years and start to get a basic understanding, we tend to be more concerned about answers and results. However, I believe that what we should really be interested in are the underlying questions.

What happened to our wonder of the things dogs do and the reasons behind their choices?

Personally, I had a renewal of childhood wonder for the character and individuality of animals and their personality through my entertaining but strenuous friendship with Chico, the little Vervet monkey who lived with me in Angola. In order to train him to do anything, I had to study his behaviour to find out his preferences and dislikes. What made him react in one way or another? After two weeks of training and living together the first and major test arose: I let him off lead. The young monkey rushed like a tiny furry blizzard to the top of a 30-40 metre high eucalyptus tree and vanished! As soon as I had regained my breath I put my plan into action.

"Chico, come!" I called. Chico gave his little scream of recognition from the tree tops before he came scurrying and jumping back to collect his strawberry!

The training methods described in this book are all free of physical punishment and unpleasantness. I prefer to plan the training so that the dog herself will choose to do what I want. Then, my challenge is to make sure it pays off well enough so that the likelihood of the dog repeating this particular behaviour increases. I do this using positive reinforcement of the desired behaviour, with treats and praise. In the art of dog training many things can happen and good contingency plans will be needed. This makes it necessary to be able to observe each dog to find out just what it is that makes this dog do as we want. Because of this you may have to make your own slight adjustments to some of my methods or "recipes" as I like to call them. A word of warning though: do not fall for the temptation of helping your dog to solve a problem. Instead, I suggest that you consider an entirely new task for your dog that is slightly

easier. It is so important to ensure that you always set your dog (and yourself) up for success!

Each chapter is written so that it can be read separately as an independent "recipe". The exception is the chapter on tracking which builds on the preceding chapter on pancake tracking.

I hope that you and your dog will have many wonderful times together as a result of reading this book.

Author's note:

In order to avoid confusion, I have referred to the dog as "she" and the handler as "he" throughout the book.

Chico

Chico, the little Vervet monkey who lived with me in Angola, helped consolidate my understanding of positive reinforcement. In a number of countries in Africa, monkey mothers are shot in order to acquire the baby clinging to the dead mother. The mother is usually eaten, and the baby sold as a pet.

Chapter 1

The sense of smell

When did you last sense the smell of water?

Troll, my dog, could smell water from a long distance. This ability is shared by animals in dry areas like deserts; otherwise they would not be able to live there.

In addition, Troll could hear water, especially when the water was a cheerful and tempting murmuring stream or a waterfall. I can hear waterfalls too, but not as far away as Troll could.

Apparently, Troll could not see people standing still in the distance. But I can. This is why a person could easily hide from Troll in the distance, just by standing motionless next to a tree or between some trees. But as soon as this person moved, Troll too was able to spot the person. One day Troll was sitting in a chair and barking whilst looking out of a closed window. None of us could see anything suspicious out there, but Troll was persistent, and eventually we could see what had caught her attention: on the slope about 80 metres away some roe deer were moving between the trees. Were it not for the white tails, none of us two legged creatures would have seen them.

All of us sharing our lives with dogs have noticed that their senses are superior to ours in many areas. But how conscious is your knowledge of your dog's senses? Do you really know how well your dog can see, smell or hear? Have you thought of the fact that your dog prioritises her senses in various circumstances?

Just like us, dogs can see, smell, hear, taste and feel, using all the senses to understand the world around them. In addition to this, many people claim to be able to communicate telepathically with dogs. In this book, I will describe some games that allow dogs to utilise their olfactory sense – the sense of smell.

Dogs have long been used to search for people lost in avalanches or bewildered in the forest. Dogs can detect landmines; many of us have heard of pigs as well as dogs finding truffles in Europe. A new revelation in our civilisation is dogs that detect cancer in human patients. The dog sniffs the patient and then marks the spot. Fantastic! A student on a camp in Canada told me that he had evidence of this taking place much earlier in history - between 4000 and 2000 years before our time. One temple had a priest, dogs and surgeons and surgery would be done once dogs had pointed out the area to investigate. Later, the temple was destroyed and the knowledge disappeared.

Sophie and Riley work as a team to find survivors of an earthquake

Many dogs have learned to find Chanterelle mushrooms for their owners, or to retrace their steps on a day's walk to fetch something that Mum "lost" on the walk. Dogs have also learned to pick out their owners' car keys from a pile of many other keys, for example.

A blind lady passed my house one day, and she told the story of her previous guide dog that occasionally would seem to prevent her from leaving the coach. After a couple of times, it appeared to happen only before she was about to have a diabetic fit. She called the guide dog school to ask how they figured out this training, only to learn that they had absolutely no idea what she was talking about. The dog had learned this all by itself. There are many similar stories about the capabilities of dogs. My experience is that the limitations of what and how to deploy the dogs' olfactory sense remain in the human brain.

Dogs need to use their senses of smell to understand the world around them. We should take time to encourage their use of all their senses.

Chapter 2

Taking advantage of natural behaviour

Have you ever considered what your dog does to please you? And also what you do to keep your dog happy?

When working with dogs we can benefit from considering their legacy from the wolf. We should remember that they prioritise their senses in order to find the "cheapest" food.

Dogs have retained most of their instincts and behaviour from their time as wild carnivores.

A wild dog or wolf's greatest concern will be staying alive. Therefore, it is essential to get hold of as much protein as possible whilst expending as little energy as necessary in order to obtain it.

Just like humans, dogs find their bearings (orientate themselves) firstly according to vision. Additionally dogs rely to a large extent upon their well-developed olfactory sense. Even so the olfactory sense will not normally be the first choice of tools when a hungry dog is searching for food. The "cheapest" food is the closest one, which means that which is within sight. If nothing edible is visible the dog or wolf will listen for potential prey. Only if neither of these two senses lead to a meal will the dog put the olfactory sense into gear. The first means of deploying the sense of smell will be to sniff the wind for any information. The last choice of ways in which to get the shopping done is to put the nose to ground and sniff for a track.

Don't forget this when you plan your training. If you want your dog to solve a task using the nose you have to eliminate any possibilities of her solving the problem by sight or hearing. Many eager dog people have had annoying experiences of how things the dog sees or hears disturbs the dog in its work.

How good is the dog's olfactory sense?

I often hear stories of male dogs that have a special awareness of when females have their season. When the bitch lives in the house nearby it is easy to understand. Every so often the bitch on heat lives far away, but still Rambo refuses to eat and sits on the veranda howling at nights.

Laboratory work referred to by Mechem® South Africa, has shown that dogs' noses are capable of

The priority of senses

1: Vision

2: Hearing

3: Olfactory

recognising molecules in as low a concentration as 10^{-18}. When I first heard this, I had no idea what it meant. The scientist who informed me of this fact was kind and understanding, and explained it for me. Imagine a beach 500 metres long, 50 metres wide and 50 centimetres deep. On this beach, a dog can find two grains of sand. Incredible, isn't it?

Dogs that I trained in Angola could find land mines buried 20 cm under the ground more than 10 years previously. A South African colleague told me of an episode where a dog marked a mine, which lay 30 metres away from where the dog was. And still we continue to wonder over Rambo's restlessness when a bitch 4km away is on heat...

In nature it is easy to imagine that the dog or wolf can sense the difference between the tracks of a moose, hare, fox, or another dog. Depending on her motivation the dog will choose one of the tracks: if she is hungry and alone she will probably track the hare; if she is hungry and has

company she may track the moose. A fed and lonely dog may choose to follow the dog track. And finally: if she is fed and satisfied, she is most likely to refrain from doing anything at all!

But what does all this have to do with our domesticated pet dogs? They have their meals served by us and don't have to exert themselves or expose themselves to danger in their search for food. And dogs always sniff around when we walk them. Isn't this sufficient?

In many cases it is not quite good enough. Many dogs get sufficient walks and exercise and maybe even training, but too little stimulation of their innate instincts. A lot of the training we do with our dogs includes speed, excitement, precision and control, but very little calm activities using concentration.

Many pupils from my earlier courses in nose work with dogs have reported back that in general their cooperation with the dog has improved, and that the relationship between dog and owner has been strengthened through the training based

Dogs are capable of finding two grains of sand on a beach that is 500 metres long by 50 metres wide and 50 centimetres deep.

upon the dog's olfactory sense. In many instances one consequence is an improvement in performance in other disciplines, such as obedience competitions. The phenomenon may be clarified by the understanding of the term "situational leadership".[1] In brief, situational leadership means that the one having the special skills needed in any situation takes the lead for the duration of that particular situation. This management structure is dynamic, and has nothing to do with who has the total responsibility or leadership in the organisation (or pack). Apparently, the system stimulates everyone in the organisation to better performance and cooperation.

So to which ends have we so far managed to take advantage of the dog's olfactory sense? People travelling internationally may have seen dogs at borders checking baggage for food, explosives or drugs. More recently we have seen that the police are using so called "corpse dogs" to prove whether there has been a dead body at a certain place or not. Both in Germany and the Netherlands courts have accepted the validity of identifying criminals by letting dogs sniff at objects found at the site of the crime.[2]

Through my work of training dogs to detect land mines, I learnt to understand a system (MEDDS® now known as the REST system) where dogs analyse air samples taken from roads, containers or cars, in order to check those samples for explosives, drugs, mines, ivory or other substances. Impressive, isn't it? People with allergies can even train their dog to verify that their food is safe to eat.

So, it appears that the limitations for our deployment of the dogs' olfactory sense remain with the human brain. We simply do not understand the full extent of the scope of this terrific tool, and thus are unable to see all possible uses.

But what about my little pet dog, I hear you asking? She is neither going to find land mines nor guard the nation's borders against illegal imports, so what does all this have to do with me? Well, both you and Tramp may have lots of fun copying some of these games and using them in your daily life. Some are simple and may be trained at home, indoors or in the garden, and others are more complex. My intention is to offer ideas for everyone. Maybe you will decide to try out more after first having tested out some of the games you find easiest.

[1] Bru and Kittelsen, 2002

[2] Kaldenbach, 1998

Jane works surrounded by explosives in Angola

Chapter 3

Points to consider before starting

- Knowledge of the dog: how dogs learn, how to make the dog happy, what limitations both you and your dog have as regards health, physical abilities or mental strength, for example.
- High value treats
- Toys
- Harness
- Short lead (around 3 metres) and a long line (7 – 12 metres) for some of the games
- Something to search for when doing scent discrimination (details will be covered in the chapter itself)

What is needed to get started?

Many people think that the priorities in quality training are the demands on the dog. I do not fully agree with this. I believe that it is most important to consider the demands on the handler. As the dog's trainer and handler you must have enough patience, be sufficiently systematic and, last but not least, be determined to reach your aim: be stubborn! The training of dogs (and other animals) is a pleasure, but it is never straightforward. You must be prepared to cope with stagnation as well as taking backward steps at least once in a while.

Having the personal skills needed, it is rarely a problem to find a suitable dog. The training methods I am about to describe are free of pain, discomfort and fear: in other words, totally harmless.

As long as your dog is healthy and has no injuries that hinder her, you can train the dog for almost anything. Not all become champions, but every dog can learn a bit of everything. Adjust your expectations and your demands on performance according to the dog's breed or type, size, age, physical and mental fitness and health.

Necessities for training

You must have:
- Patience
- The ability to be systematic
- Sufficient motivation and enough stubbornness to stick to the plan

Plan your training

It is the very first track, the first drug-sniffer dog's search for hashish, the first search and rescue dog's search for a lost person or the first mushroom search; any first search is the most important one in the dog's life! The way the dog solves a task the first time will be the chosen method later in life when the dog meets problems in a similar situation, no matter how many months or years of training that lie between. Do not begin your training without having carefully thought through what you want to achieve, and without having made a plan.

If you have not planned the training thoroughly it is better to delay the training for now and go for a nice walk instead.

How dogs learn

Dogs learn by association. This means connecting one event or object with another. As humans, we make associations too: when I see a travel brochure, I immediately start to dream of holidays I have been on or would like to enjoy. Seeing someone grabbing their car keys, I assume they are about to leave. Dogs think about things in a similar way. Many dogs know the difference between an office coat and a leisure coat. Your dog has probably learnt to associate being taken for a walk whenever you use a certain coat.

Numerous dogs have learnt the meaning of certain words without us teaching them: typical examples are "food" and "walk". When teaching a dog a new trick, I am conscious about when I apply the cue (a word or action that will eventually prompt the dog to perform the behaviour I want). For instance, in teaching 'sit' I hold a treat over the dog's nose, and only when the dog sits will she get the treat. After a couple of repetitions the dog will associate a treat above her nose with sitting. I never give the cue at this early stage. When you know your dog will perform the behaviour you want, it is time to give the behaviour a name.

In my way of training, it is vital that the dog forms only positive associations as I cannot afford for the dog to be worried or stressed and make a mistake as a result. My dog will work together with me because she wants to. Force or so-called punishment is something I never apply. However, I can remove the opportunity for the dog to be reinforced, i.e. take away a treat (negative punishment) if the dog does not perform. I will give the dog something she likes, (positive reinforcement), to pay for good behaviour.

The word "no", or other forms of negative reaction are completely inadvisable during the training of dogs, whether it be obedience, searching for bombs or agility training. When you say "No!" or jerk on the lead or do anything else to correct the dog, this will cause a negative feeling in the dog. Negative feelings are learnt more strongly and quickly than the positive ones, so it does not help much to praise the dog for doing the right thing immediately after the correction. The negative impact is already in place

and will often leave the dog stressed or insecure and unable to think clearly.

This mouse finds that payment for work can be really motivating!

Motivation

To ensure that your dog is willing to work for you at any time, it is crucial that she has sufficient motivation. Correct motivation is achieved through giving the right amount of the right reinforcement at the right time. As Aristotle said: "Anybody can become angry. That is easy; but to be angry with the right person, and to the right degree, and at the right time, and for the right purpose, and in the right way, that is not within everybody's power and is not easy".

An alternative way of looking at this would be to say that giving a sufficiently good payment or reward at the right time to reinforce the desired behaviour in your dog is both a science and an art. Mastering this will make you a really good animal trainer.

Sometimes the dog's "payment" must be the best it can possibly be. At other times, all that is needed is a pleasant word from you. You, yourself must learn to recognise which performances should be paid for and by which means. Myself, I follow the simple rule that I pay with the very best for a surprisingly good performance; for a normally good performance, I pay with something that holds a little lower value and for a performance of an expected quality, I might just give verbal praise.

Remember to pay attention to your own motivation as well. If you want progress in the training, both you and the dog must receive rewards that are worth the effort!

Food as reward/reinforcement

Food is my preferred reward when teaching something new. Food is the ultimate reward for all who live and eat. Any exertion from an adult wild predator will mainly be to get food, to survive.

Treats for training must be small, fresh and juicy, providing tasty and quickly eaten reinforcements. I want to avoid a situation where biscuits make crumbs and the dog ends up searching the ground for more goodies whilst I wait for her to be ready to continue the training. Neither do I want a situation to arise where I pay with a ball and the dog runs off to play with the ball leaving me behind. Reinforcement with objects (toys) often takes too long for initial learning, and moves focus from the training to play. Additionally toys as rewards always finish with a "negative" experience, as you often have to take the object from the dog either by force or by command.

The Seven Wonders of the World

Do you *really* know what your dog likes the best? I remember reading a story about a polar bear being trained. Imagine this situation. What would you use as treats? Fish, meat, fat? Good thinking, but not this time. This polar bear's favourite was raisins.

The favourite treat of a Labrador Retriever I once met was cucumber. However, most dogs prefer something from the butcher of course, or perhaps fish or cheese.

To make a ranking list of what your dog likes the most, collect the items you want to test. If it is food, take a small piece of liver in one hand for example, and chicken in the other. Close your hands and let the dog sniff at them to find out what they contain before you hold your hands a little further away from each other. The hand your dog is most interested in will contain the best treat of these two. Perhaps the chicken won over the liver. Make a note of the result, and carry on comparing chicken to all the other things, fish cakes, cheese, hot dog, waffle or whatever.

Compare each treat with all the others, until you have a ranking list of your dog's "Seven Wonders of the Treat World". This list is your tool for picking the right payment in different situations. If your dog has a very low motivation, use a high ranking treat to surprise her. Likewise, if the dog's performance has been very good, pick a high ranking treat. If the performance is acceptable but not special, pick a treat from the bottom of the list.

Variable reinforcement

In addition to varying the treats, I use variable reinforcement. Variable reinforcement means simply that the dog never knows beforehand whether she will receive a treat. The idea is that your dog gets a treat every time initially, until she starts to understand what you want. Then you give a treat every second time until the dog gets better. When the dog is becoming reliable (80% performance), you start treating every 3-8 times on a random basis, which is variable reinforcement. You continue with variable reinforcement forever. Of course, you can praise every time, but be mean with the treats. The point is that the dog should not know when a treat will come, nor what she is likely to receive. In this way you will sustain the dog's excitement for the work. Compare it with a slot machine: there is always some anticipation, whilst on the other hand a vending machine is rather too predictable.

Jackpot

Each time your dog performs extremely well, you can give a jackpot. It is easiest to have sufficient treats in your hand/pocket for 5-6 repetitions. When the dog has a breakthrough, I give what I have left in my hand as the jackpot. A jackpot may also be something totally different. If you train using food as reinforcement, a toy may be the jackpot. If the dog is allowed the freedom to do something of her own choice, this may also be a good jackpot. For Tan, the mine detection dog, the best jackpot he could have was to play in water. Once my dog came back (unexpectedly!) when called from chasing a cat but I had neither

Tan playing in water is a quality reward for an excellent performance

This jackpot consists of one whole chicken!

a toy nor a treat and really did not know how to pay my dog for this wonderful behaviour. At the last minute, I realised that I always have myself, so I improvised and acted the clown by throwing myself on the ground, turning somersaults in the heather, laughing, playing and petting her. And guess what: it worked! You may be inventive in creating good reinforcements, but don't forget your own voice and body. This is what you always have available in any situation.

A jackpot is meant to be a quality reward for your dog. The jackpot's magic is to be seldom utilised and only for special efforts on the dog's part. A jackpot loses its effect if used too frequently.

Shaping and clicker training

As you will see from my descriptions, my methods are very much like shaping. My personal experience is that clicker training is well suited for training specifics like scent discrimination (such as searching for a Chanterelle mushroom).

It is beyond the aim of this book to cover shaping and clicker training. However, if your dog is clicker trained, you can use the clicker for many of the exercises I describe in the book.

The training itself

Before you start, bear in mind the importance of not overdoing the training. Never make too many repetitions in a row. Again, I have a golden rule for training new behaviours: do a maximum of five repetitions, and then take a short break before doing another 1-5 repetitions. Stop when the dog has done something good. The short break needs be only a few seconds or minutes.

If you complete five trials without any success, treat the dog anyway (for being so patient with you!), and then figure out what is going wrong. Were there too many distractions; was the dog ill, very tired or had she been fed recently? Were you grumpy, or was it simply too difficult for the dog for any reason?

If your dog performs perfectly on trial number 1, give a jackpot and take a short break. Always end the training session with the best you can expect. This establishes a positive learning experience, leading to having a dog that comes to training sessions with joy. Whenever you have completed 3-5 sessions (of 1-5 repetitions), you need a longer break of 10 minutes or more. In some cases your break might last for hours or days, depending upon what you are training. The duration and frequency of the break must be adjusted according to the dog in question and when she starts to be tired. Ideally you should stop before the dog's interest begins to sink.

During the course of a day you may have many small training sessions as long as you make sure you give breaks when needed.

Setting the dog up for success is your responsibility.

Taking a break

It may seem rather paradoxical to begin a book on dog training by describing what constitutes a break.

I am including it here because I have experienced that one of the most critical parts of dog training is the breaks. What I do with my dog (and myself!) in the break, what the duration of the break is, and when to take a break are all crucial questions.

Have a break!

What is the purpose of a break?

One way of looking at taking a break is that it is a time for both you and your dog to rest, relax, digest what is learnt and get ready for doing more afterwards. It is important that you are aware of what is relaxing for your dog and what is not. Dogs are all different. Many dogs enjoy a nice rest in the car. Others will be hysterical about being left alone in the car, or they may feel that it is their duty to guard it and as a result they will be in work mode all the time, not resting at all, even if nobody comes close to the car.

In classes I often see that the dog owners use the breaks to train something else, like obedience, tricks, agility obstacles or whatever. This is normally a very bad idea. When you train something else in the break, you remove from the dog's memory all thoughts of what she just did, and replace it with the consciousness of what she is doing now. If more training follows a task that is being trained it is not a break anyway.

Playing with other dogs or running freely around is also often looked on by owners as an intermission given with the best of intentions. Normally this is not a good idea, either. This also moves the focus of the training, and is not really relaxing.

I recommend strolling with the dog on lead, letting her sniff where she wants. If the training has been lengthy incorporating a great deal of thought and problem solving, a little jogging may be good. On the other hand, if the training has been very active with a great deal of speed and action, a calm stroll or a doze in the car or in the shade may be the best thing to do. But do not go straight from high activity to having a rest: remember to cool the dog down first by allowing a few minutes of slow walking, letting the dog sniff around. Learn from athletes and horse riders: warm up first and cool down afterwards!

When should you take a break?

Mostly, this will be long before you think you need one! You should take a break whilst the training is still progressing, providing that both you and your dog remember the session as being positive. It may be that your dog performs very well on the first try. Fine - praise and treat and take a short break before carrying on with the same task. A short break may be only 20 seconds, or it may be more. We humans tend to think "Wow, we have really made progress, this is fun, let's do it just one more time!" - and then of course, it goes wrong. Stop in time! Stop when the dog's interest (or yours) is at its peak; if it has begun to wane, you should have already taken a break. During training you should begin to learn the best time to take a break.

When do I leave one step for the next?

Another golden rule is to move on when we have 80% performance. A long time ago I was told that we had to get a dog to perform at least 80 - 100 repetitions of a trick before the dog had learnt it. Fortunately, we now know better. These dogs must have been frustrated or bored with such slow progress. For some adult dogs that are fast learners, it is too much to follow the 80% rule, as to measure this we have to do five repetitions, and this can be too much. I have seen dogs that understand the point of the training after the first or second time. Bright dogs can easily lose interest if we carry on cramming. By raising the criteria, these dogs' interest will be more likely to reawaken.

The most frequent reason for training problems is trying to proceed too quickly. On the other hand I have found that the second most frequent reason for problems is progress that is too slow. Find the balance of progression for you and your dog, and you will avoid unnecessary frustration. Both of you will have much more fun!

Chapter 4

Search for treats

This is a game your dog can play with children or adults, indoors or outdoors, in the garden or in the fields or woods.

Hide a variety of different sized treats around the house, garden or somewhere in the woods. Then, let your dog sniff them all out! Your dog will be searching all alone without having seen what you did, and without any help from you or anybody else. This searching may last quite a while, as long as your dog is totally satisfied and ready for some rest afterwards. You may not think this is possible for you and your dog. Hopefully, after reading these few pages you will see that it is less complicated than you thought.

By nature, dogs have to use a combination of their nose, brain and legs in order to search for food (or something else they want). This is what we take advantage of in search work competitions or search & rescue tasks.

First, we make it all as basic as possible: let the dog search for something that she will be really happy to find, and allow her to receive the reward immediately on the spot where it was found.

All dog owners I have spoken to find this game easy and amusing for both dog and human. Most dogs find great satisfaction in searching and finding food, and a dog that is good at this may search a huge area in order to find many little edible surprises. You will see how your dog becomes calmer and more contented after this work. A session of searching for treats is far more stimulating than jogging or obedience training.

If you would like your dog to learn the search square later on (see page 32), but she does not yet retrieve, searching for treats may be a good thing to train in the mean time. This will help your dog to learn to search eagerly and meticulously.

You should give your dog a certain cue (or a signal to work) for finding food: "find your treats", for instance. In this way, you will eliminate any future confusion in search square work which will have a different cue ("square" for example). One advantage of using little treats is that if the dog does not find them all, you can leave them for the ants or mice!

The first time you teach your dog to search for treats, hold her on lead. It does not matter whether you are inside or outdoors. Make sure that your dog is not told to "sit", "down", or "wait", and is not given any other cue: simply hold the lead. Place yourself along with the dog so that she is looking in the same direction as you, and throw a couple of treats no further than one metre away, giving your dog every opportunity to see where they land. Immediately release the dog so that she can chase after the treats. At this point you should not yet be giving a cue. Only later, when your dog has understood what this is all about, do you introduce the cue. As I said, you can train this wherever you want, the recipe is the same. The only difference is that the size of the search area is much more limited indoors...

The training steps are as follows:
Step 1

* Throw a couple of treats, no more than one metre away whilst the dog is watching.

* Once the treats have landed, let the dog run to find them.

* Join in the celebrations by praising your dog, telling her how wonderful a search dog she is.

* As the last treat is swallowed, call your dog back to you.

* Repeat this process a couple of times.

Remember that dogs learn faster than you think, so be prepared to increase the challenge within a very short space of time.

Step 2:

☙ Toss two or three treats one at a time, each immediately after the other. Make sure the dog is watching and that the treats land fairly close to each other.

☙ Without any cue, let the dog run out and eat the treats.

☙ Join in the celebrations when the dog finds the treat.

☙ If the dog finds only one, call her back and toss a few new ones in the same area. In this way, the forgotten treats will become bonuses in the following search. The more treats she finds, the more amusing she will find this game, and the more successful she will find the experience.

☙ Repeat this procedure between one to three more times.

Step 3:

☙ Toss 4-5 treats, in the same way as above, only this time increase the distance from you to the treats, and also the distance between the treats.

As you have done this so many times now, your dog is probably beginning to recognise this game. Therefore you can increase these distances and still be successful.

☙ Continue to release your dog without giving any cue. Repeat this 1-3 times.

Step 4

This is the time to introduce the cue.

☙ Toss two or three treats only.

☙ Allow your dog to search for them.

☙ If your dog goes straight out to search the first time, give the cue the second time you do this. If not, go back to step 3.

Your cue might be "get the treats" or something else of your choice.

☙ Say the cue immediately before you release the dog for the search.

☙ If your dog does this well, you can give the cue every time from now on.

After a few repetitions, she will associate the cue with this game.

Take a Break

If you have done all this in one go, you need to give your dog a major break now. She will need a minimum of 10 minutes, allowing her to sniff, walk, have water and to rest. If she appears tired, make the break really long, allowing her to sleep, maybe even waiting until the following day before continuing. If you decide to have a break overnight, return to step 4 before resuming your training, otherwise go directly to step 5.

Step 5

☙ Toss even more treats, around 8-10.

☙ Each time throw them increasingly further away and with a greater distance between them.

☙ Give the cue "get your treats" at the same time as you release the dog.

☙ Repeat between one and five times.

Step 6

At this point it is high time to increase the size of the search area.

☙ If your dog knows the sit or stay cues, she can sit and watch you whilst you are preparing the task.

☙ Several treats, at least 10, are spread around to the left and right all over the area.

☙ The area may be as big as 10 x 10 metres, or even bigger if your dog is long legged

If the dog does not know the sit or stay cues, you can tie her to something safe, or preferably ask someone she knows well to help you either by holding her or placing the treats on the ground.

In the event that your dog is very stressed or whining when you place the treats, it may be better that you hold her while the helper spreads them on the ground.

Take a Break

If you have not already had time out, this is definitely the time for a major break. It is vital that the dog relaxes totally, without doing anything. Go for a little walk, unwind indoors, do whatever it takes for your dog to relax. The break should last for at least half an hour. Again, if your break lasts over night, go back one step, or even two or three steps from the step you last completed. Otherwise, continue to step 7.

Step 7

This step involves teaching the dog to do the same thing as in step 6 without watching you (or the helper) prepare the search area.

Devise a search for treats that the dog is unable to watch.

☙ Whilst the dog waits, perhaps indoors, in another room, in the car or behind a mound or rise for example, place some treats in the area you have chosen as a search area.

☙ Make it easy this time: place the treats where you expect your dog to find them easily and quickly.

☙ Bring your dog to the search area, hold her as you have done previously, give the cue "get your treats" and release her.

☙ If she starts searching now, you will be quite sure that she understands the cue, and you have achieved your goal. Congratulations!

☙ If she is unsure of what to do, repeat step 6 two or three times before trying step 7 again. No harm done! Move on to testing at step 7, returning to step 6 if your dog is still uncertain, repeating until she starts searching at the given cue.

Step 8

Adding further challenges.

☙ Now you are at the stage where you can increase the size of the search area even more. Gradually increase little by little until your search area reaches the size that is appropriate for you and your dog. To give you some idea of what kind of size area is appropriate, consider the size of your dog, her speed and how fast she works. It should be no problem for a fit Labrador or setter to search an area the size of a football pitch. Most people will be satisfied with a much smaller area, however. A field may be the perfect spot, or a calm corner in the park or a car park.

☙ You may like to vary how long the treats are lying there before the search begins. Sometimes it is easier to find "old" treats, sometimes it is more difficult. Play and experiment to find out what your dog can cope with. Make it a game between you, or between the children and your dog. The point of the game is to hide the treats, making it a real challenge for the dog to find them. Repeat at least once per week for the rest of your dog's life.

☙ Generalise the search. This means that your dog can learn to search in all types of environments, indoors or outdoors. If you began your training in a particular room, expand it now so that your dog is given the opportunity to search through more and more rooms, possibly in other houses, and also in the garden and/or the park or woods. Vary the type of woods, the type of field, the height of the grass and the type of vegetation, for example. Play this game in any possible and even improbable places, and you will see how interesting your dog finds these challenges.

In the beginning you must always ensure that you end this game whilst your dog still wants more. If you continue until the dog gets tired she may lose interest in the activity. It is especially crucial to remember this in the beginning whilst your dog is still learning what to do. Later on, when the dog knows the game and really enjoys it, you can let her work until she ends it of her own accord.

During the initial training of this game, I train at the same spot in each single session, whether it be indoors or out. Then, if the dog does not find all the treats in a search, they remain there as a bonus for the following searches. The next time your dog will receive more reinforcements, and may even learn the game faster.

If for any reason your dog does not find the hidden treats, do not show her where they are. Let them stay where they are, and after the training is over you can either remove them or leave them for other animals.

This kind of activity is extremely unlikely to teach your dog to scavenge, particularly if you put it on cue.

The little Dachshund in Japan

I would like to share with you the story about how a little Dachshund I once met learnt to use her nose.

In Japan, most small pet dogs are lap dogs, carried in the owner's arms and spending their time indoors and in the garden. That was also the case for this little Dachshund. She was an adult, and yet had no experience of using her nose for anything.

We devised a task where treats were placed on the ground 2-3 metres away from her with the little dog watching all the time. However, when she was supposed to start searching she remained fixed in position: standing and sniffing the ground immediately around her. Not until we cut the distance down to 30 centimetres did she get the point with this. And then she really understood, and searched very thoroughly and eagerly. She found all the tiny treats underneath the dead leaves, and chewed them happily. During 2-3 training sessions we more than doubled the search length. What joy for a little dog to at last feel she could use her instinctive behaviour!

Chapter 5
Hide and seek

When you start this training it is important that you choose a toy (or other object) that your dog enjoys having in her mouth, and which she will pick up all by herself just for the fun of it. With further training your dog will learn to willingly pick up all sorts of objects.

Just as with the search for treats, hide and seek may be trained indoors, in the garden or out in the woods. However, a word of warning! If the object is something you don't want to lose, bear in mind that it is important to remember where it is! This of course is in case your dog does not find the hidden object... you may just have to find it and pick it up yourself!

I wonder if you remember the game of hide and seek from your childhood? It is a game that is not difficult to teach your dog.

Dogs that enjoy carrying things in their mouth find this activity just as much fun as finding treats. The game is also suitable for children to play with the dog.

Hide and seek is very similar to searching for treats described above, the main difference being that the dog finds objects rather than food.

For this activity you will need a toy or something else that your dog loves and will enjoy holding in her mouth. It does not really matter whether or not the dog returns to you with the toy: the point is simply to search for it and find it by using the nose. If your dog finds the toy and strolls off to enjoy it alone by herself, it does not matter at this point. If my dog is unlikely to want to come back to me with her treasure, I personally would tend to play this game in a secure environment, within the boundary of walls or a fence.

If you would like to train this activity even if your dog does not retrieve (carry things in her mouth), look up how to work on this aspect in the chapter about retrieving - page 87. Here you will find a nice method of training your dog to retrieve reliably. Any dogs that have learnt to retrieve will play this game, ending it by coming back to you to give you the toy. Then you can either hide it again, exchange it with praise or a treat, or give it back to your dog to play with.

The steps of the training can be planned and carried out like this:

Step 1

🐾 Throw a toy in front of the dog whilst she is watching, let her run and find it straight away.

🐾 Share your dog's joy when she finds it.

🐾 If your dog happens to come to you with the object, give a treat and play with your dog and the object. For tips on playing with your dog see the section entitled "Naming your dog's toys" on page 26.

🐾 Repeat this 2-4 times.

Most dogs learn faster than we believe; therefore it is important to quickly increase the challenge for your dog. Always make it a little more difficult for her each time you do this.

Making mistakes or "failure"

If the dog doesn't find the object, or doesn't complete one of any of the tasks at any stage, we need to consider what is happening.

If she makes a mistake it's because we have got it wrong. We may not have been paying attention to her and she may either be too stressed or we have asked her to do a task that is too difficult for her. Therefore we should take a break at this point. However, our initial reaction should be to ignore her. Give her no negative attention, and do not help her by pointing out the toy.

Step 2

☙ Now throw the object a little further, possibly even so that it lands hidden behind something, out of sight of the dog. However, your dog will still need to see roughly where the toy lands.

☙ Once the toy has landed, release the dog in order for her to run forward towards the toy. Remember that you are still not giving any cue yet!

☙ As always: share the dog's joy by offering cheerful words when she finds the object.

☙ Repeat 2-3 times

Now it is probably time to give your dog a break of a few minutes. After the break, warm up with step 2 before continuing to step 3.

Step 3

☙ Ask your dog to sit and stay if she knows this, and go just out of range of your dog's vision before you put the object down on the ground.

☙ Return immediately to the dog and let her run out to find the object. If she does not know sit/stay, you may restrain her by tying the lead to something safe or by having someone hold her for you. If inside you could simply leave her in another room, closing the door between you.

☙ As always, celebrate when your dog finds the object and exchange with a treat if your dog comes to you with the missing treasure!

☙ Repeat the procedure 1-3 times.

Step 4

Now it is probably time to increase the size of the search area.

☙ Again, ask your dog to sit/stay or restrain her.

☙ Go out of the dog's sight and hide the object without making it too difficult.

☙ Walk about a little after laying down the object to avoid the dog following your scent to the object (and to avoid giving her too many clues as to where you have hidden it!).

☙ Allow your dog to find the object and celebrate when found.

☙ Repeat this 2-5 times.

Step 5

Now for the cue.

☙ Tell the dog the name of this game. Say "hide-and-seek" or something else of your choice and immediately release your dog to search for the object.

☙ If you feel absolutely convinced that your dog will search in step 3, you could start giving the cue at that stage. **BUT:** be careful not to give the cue unless you are absolutely sure the dog will get it right. As always, praise and treat.

☙ Repeat this 2-5 times.

So, now it's time for a time-out again. Let the dog relax totally, doing nothing. Go for a little walk, relax indoors, or do whatever is right for your dog to become calm. The next training session may be half an hour later, several hours later, or even the next day. If you wait until the next day start first at step 3 just to see what the dog remembers. Then work through steps 4-5 before you let the dog do the activity without having seen you go and hide.

Step 6

* Hide a toy when the dog cannot see you.

* The dog should be sitting indoors, in another room, in the car or behind a mound or the house, depending on where you are.

* Hide a toy that is very precious to your dog, but don't make it too difficult to find this time as you don't want the dog to give up before finding it.

* Get your dog, hold her as you did before, give the cue "hide-and-seek" and let her go.

* If she starts to search now, you know she understands the cue and you have achieved your goal! Congratulations!

If she does not find the toy, repeat step 5 two-three times and test with step 6 again. Continue repeating steps 5-6 until your dog starts to search on the given cue.

Step 7

* Make the search area even larger and more difficult.

* If you are playing this game indoors, hide the object behind furniture, under carpets, on a shelf, between the cushions - use your imagination. However, only hide things where your dog is allowed to go!

* You can walk through several rooms if playing indoors, or if outdoors, let the area be 30-50 metres wide. But increase the size gradually, starting with 10 metres, then 15 or 20 etc.

Step 8

* Vary how long the object has stayed hidden. Some times it is easier to find objects that have been hidden for a while as their scent has had time to become established.

Take a Break

* Play and experiment to find out what your dog masters, and make this a game between you and your dog, or the children and the dog.

When training this, just as with any other training, always make sure you stop whilst your dog still wants more! If you carry on until she gets tired, she may lose interest in this game. It is important to bear this in mind especially in the beginning when the learning starts, later, when the dog knows the game and likes it too, you may let her work until she gives up now and again.

For some dogs there is only one object they are willing to search for; for other dogs you might make a point of changing the object every so often so it is not always the same.

An amusing variation:

If you remember the hide-and-seek game correctly, you may have noticed something missing: we used to call out "hotter" when the searcher got nearer to the object, and "colder" when the searcher moved away from the hiding place.

We can also teach this to our dogs. As the dog gets used to the activity you can say "hotter" every time she gets close and upon hearing this word your dog will begin to intensify the search.

Before adding this refinement, I do recommend that you take your dog through all the steps first however, in order to ensure she understands the meaning of the game.

Dirham and the purse...

Many years ago I had a Tervueren named Dirham who was certified as a search and rescue dog in the Association of Norwegian Search & Rescue dogs. He enjoyed finding things that people had "lost", which he was trained to do on my signal. Once, as we were walking through my town, he insisted on investigating a narrow stretch of shrubbery by the footpath. I had learnt to trust him, so I let him loose. After rummaging in the shrubbery for a short while, he came out with a handbag between his jaws, and something similar to a big smile on his face. The handbag no longer contained any money, but was someone's personal property. I gave it to the police. The day after I was informed that the handbag belonged to an old lady who had been robbed some days before, and she was very happy to get back her handbag and its remaining contents, including her old Bible.

Chapter 6

Naming your dog's toys

A charming variation of hide and seek or the search square, is to teach your dog to search for a particular toy or object. Somewhere in the house (or the garden or woods) place "Teddy", for example, and ask your dog to go and find it. The dog searches through the entire house, passing all the other toys on her way: but on this occasion it is only Teddy that counts, and nothing else. Teddy has either been hidden by you, or it just remains where it was left when it was last played with.

This is the aim, and although there is some work to do prior to achieving this, it is nowhere near as difficult as it might seem in the first place. Follow my "recipe" and you will see that your dog learns this faster than you would believe.

Choose a toy or another item that your dog really likes, and use this through all the initial training. Only when your dog is sure about finding this item is it time to teach the name of another object. In this book we will begin with a teddy bear as an example, but you can use whichever item you would like to of course.

Step 1

👣 Hold Teddy in front of your dog and invite your dog to take it by moving it around at floor level and playing with the object. Do not say anything at this stage.

👣 Once she grabs it, say "Teddy" in a pleasant, encouraging way, then praise and play as a reward.

👣 Repeat this 2-5 times.

Step 2

👣 Now, instead of holding Teddy in your hand, place Teddy on the floor.

👣 If your dog does not take it by herself, invite her to grab Teddy by playing cat & mouse with your dog. This game involves moving Teddy on the floor using small rapid movements to encourage interest.

👣 The instant your dog grabs Teddy, say: "Teddy" and praise and play again.

👣 Repeat this 1-5 times in a row.

Step 3

Now you can try some small tests to check your dog's understanding: hold the dog gently by the collar, place Teddy on the floor out of your dog's reach, ensuring she is able to see Teddy. Now release the dog and say "Teddy". Once the dog starts to move towards Teddy, praise and play. After repeating this 2-5 times your dog has probably understood the cue.

If you trained these three steps in a row, you will need to take a break of at least 10 minutes now.

If your dog does not go towards Teddy, she may be tired or distracted. In this case, take a break and start again!

After the break, start with something slightly easier than the task you finished with in order to warm up. When the warm up progresses smoothly, carry on quickly through all the steps after that. You will be ready for the next step once your dog starts to move on your cue of "Teddy".

Step 4

It is now time to place Teddy out of sight of your dog.

👣 Show Teddy to your dog (who is either tied, in a sit-stay or is being held by someone).

☻ Go and hide Teddy behind the door or a chair making sure she cannot see it from where she is.

☻ Go back to the dog, let her go and give her lots of praise when she finds Teddy. I do not recommend giving the cue the first time you hide Teddy out of sight.

☻ Regard the first hiding as a test, and if this works well add the cue the second time.

☻ Remember, always praise your dog for successes by sharing the joy when she finds Teddy.

☻ Repeat 1-5 times.

Step 5

☻ Now you can increase the difficulty of the task: hide Teddy so that Teddy is not visible unless the dog searches a little bit.

☻ Teddy may be under a cushion, between legs of furniture or something similar, so that your dog really has to use her nose to find Teddy. However, you should not make it too complicated as you do not want your dog to give up. The difficulty of this task must be increased only gradually. If it was too difficult for your dog, give her a new task easy enough to master, praise a lot and take a break. Never ever be tempted to help your dog to solve the problem. If you do, you will only teach her that it pays to give up.

☻ Repeat 1-5 times.

Time for that break!

Take a Break

Step 6

Now you can test that your dog understands the difference between Teddy and the other toys.

☻ Place Teddy on the floor along with one or two other toys. Teddy should be closest to your dog and you should ensure that all items are visible to your dog.

☸ Say "Teddy", and let the dog loose to work by herself. If she chooses correctly, you have achieved your aim: congratulations!

☸ If she picks the wrong toy, ignore this and go back to step 3, working forward through the steps once more.

☸ Whenever your dog touches one of the other toys, look the other way, and do not receive this one if she wants to give it to you. If you are lucky your dog will then leave this toy and go back to searching. If she now picks Teddy, celebrate! It is birthday and Christmas at the same time! Give a jackpot, and take a break.

☸ Repeat this step, varying the position of the Teddy between the others items, until your dog reliably picks Teddy and ignores anything else. But again: ensure you do no more than 1-5 repetitions in a row.

Take a Break

Step 7

Now your dog knows the name of Teddy, start to hide more toys in the house including Teddy, in increasingly difficult places.

Ask your dog to find Teddy, and celebrate whenever she finds Teddy. If there are any mistakes return to step 6.

Step 8

If you wish to take this trick even further, take Teddy and the other toys into other environments.

Go through all the steps in each new environment. You can go anywhere: garden, the park, the woods, a meadow, to a friend's house, the dog club, etc. and you will find that the training progresses more quickly in each new environment you go to.

Step 9

Once your dog has reliably learnt who Teddy is, teach her the name of other toys, one by one,

following the same recipe. Choose names of toys that **sound** different, not only ones that have a different meaning.

It may be difficult for your dog to ignore Teddy in the early stages of teaching the names of other new toys (in step 6). Use "neutral" toys first (toys that do not yet have a name and that are not very interesting to your dog).

Stage 10

When the new name of an item is fully learnt, for example "Ball", you can start to teach the difference between Teddy and Ball.

Ensure you only make a very few repetitions, and stop before your dog gets confused. Very often one repetition is enough at this stage!

Another method of teaching your dog the name of toys, which is just as effective, is simply to watch when she takes a toy in her mouth. The instant she grabs the toy, say the name of the item, praise her, and play with it. After several repetitions the dog will soon learn the names of "Ball", "Teddy", or even "The Red One", for example.

In addition, you can even teach your dog the name of your slippers, for example. Imagine having a dog that gets your slippers when asked!

During a workshop in Germany in autumn 2003, the students reported a story of a dog that had recently been on German TV. A young Border Collie had been injured and had to be kept calm for a few months while recuperating. Not a very easy task... However, the owners found a way to keep him calm yet occupied: they trained the dog to use his brain instead of his legs. Dogs get just as tired from thinking as from running. This young Border Collie learnt the name of all his toys and many other items. Eventually he had learnt the name of almost 100 toys.

Chapter 7
Search Square

An area of 50m x 50m is an ideal size to teach your dog to search systematically for lost items

This is the art of searching for things that we humans have lost!

It can be a competitive sport for some, deadly serious for others and a source of amusement for most. The term for setting up a specific area with hidden items for the dog to find is a search square.

Your dog sniffs systematically along the ground on a "pathway" immediately in front of the spot in which you are standing. She runs and works eagerly, reaches a distance of 50 metres where she turns and comes back to you. You praise her, move a few steps sideways and your dog runs out searching again. Once more she runs to 50 metres before turning around. On the way back she becomes more alert, and runs a few metres to the side, sticks her head into the heather and then comes rushing back to you. In her mouth she holds a tiny piece of cloth that she wants to give you! She has realised that you become very happy when she does things like this. She is just as happy as you are, as she is overjoyed with the chicken neck with which you pay her.

In this way, you and your dog will search the field of 50 x 50 metres and you will have a full overview of which part of the field has been searched and which has not. No corner or secret place will be forgotten, something which could lead to losing points if this were a competition.

When training the search square the best results are achieved by breaking the training up into several steps. Patience is essential, along with systematic and optimal reinforcements for the dog.

Many find me too much of a control freak when I wish to have so much influence in dictating where in the field the dog is searching. Maybe they are right. I got into this habit during my years of training dogs to find land mines. There is simply no alternative to finding everything and covering the whole area when searching for landmines, as this can be a matter of life and death. When I saw how well searching in this way worked, I simply adjusted the minefield system to a bigger and rougher search.

As always, I have split the training into small steps. Each step contains an aim, a separate milestone. In order to have a dog that is fully trained for the search square I have divided the way forward into eight steps:

🐾 Establish and build up the dog's motivation for searching

🐾 Cement the dog's understanding that it is fun to find pathways pointing straight ahead from the direction in which Mum or Dad are facing, and to train the dog to search all the way to 50 metres.

🐾 Teach the dog to search on a certain cue.

🐾 Teach the dog to search without being motivated by the sight of an item.

🐾 Teach the dog to search whether there is a "pathway" of scent or not.

🐾 Describe how to get the dog to search from the very first step and then all the way out to 50 metres.

🐾 Build up the dog's belief that when she does not find anything, there will be something next time she hears the cue.

🐾 Generalise the search to be accurate in all kinds of environments.

At this point you have achieved your aim!

Teaching the search square

To begin with, you need very good treats, some object your dog loves dearly, and preferably a helper. You will need to take these with you to a fairly peaceful place without too many distractions where the training can begin.

Actually, the training started some time ago, because your dog already knows how to retrieve. (See the chapter on retrieving later on in this book). In the event that your dog does not want to retrieve, you may follow the steps described and use treats instead of objects. Using treats for objects may be carried out for a period, whilst intensively training the retrieve in parallel.

In the initial training phase I prefer the reward to be exchanging the object with a highly treasured treat rather than playing, as playing removes the focus from what we are actually training. Once the dog is more experienced in the game, I may start to play with the objects as a variation (or addition) to the treats.

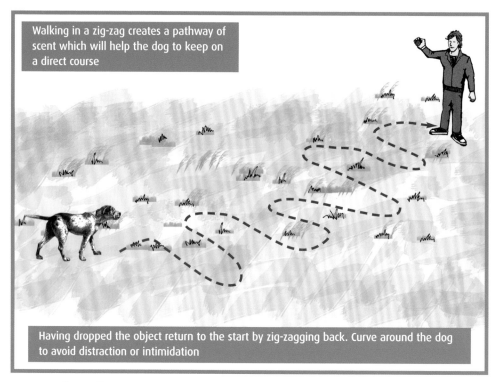

Walking in a zig-zag creates a pathway of scent which will help the dog to keep on a direct course

Having dropped the object return to the start by zig-zagging back. Curve around the dog to avoid distraction or intimidation

Stage1. The willingness to search

As it is the dog's desire to work that is the main purpose of this stage, it is crucial that what the dog finds really is exciting for her. It is not sufficient that it is merely something that your dog is "willing to take".

🐾 Tie your dog to a tree or hold her on lead.

🐾 Next, you (or the helper) should go out creating a pathway of scent by running in a zigzag at a width of 3-4 metres. Make it no more than 10-20 metres long the first time.

🐾 Make sure your dog sees what you or the helper has done, without making too much fuss about it. Be aware how difficult it is to keep the direction whilst running in a zigzag! Your dog should always be watching.

🐾 At the end of the zigzag, drop the object – a glove or toy or whatever you have – and zigzag back. This way you create a pathway of scent, which is meant to help your dog keep on a direct course to the glove, despite there being no real track to it.

🐾 The first few times you let the dog go for the glove, do so without giving any cue.

🐾 When your dog finds the glove, praise, and when she comes to you with the object change it for the treat. Be ready with the treat, don't let the dog wait for it!

In the beginning it is really important that the object indicates that when she finds the item there will be a real celebration for her. Finding the object must be fun in itself, and in the beginning it is really important that your dog feels that the best thing she can do is to find it! Troll, my standard poodle was really excited by one of my gloves, for example, whereas other dogs will be absolutely thrilled by finding a squeaky toy, ball, a ragger or a child's toy. Know your own dog and use what she likes the best.

🐾 Repeat this 1-5 times before taking a break. As always: stop with the best you can expect. And also remember to stop while the dog still wants more.

Send the dog to find the object, initially with no cue. Praise when the dog returns with the object

Use the same "scent" highway again and again

I always use the same pathway of scent in the beginning as this makes it easier for the dog to stick to the straight forward search pattern.

If you are having any problems with your dog not giving the object nicely back to you, do not train a retrieve at this point. The specifics of retrieve training can be trained better at home before applying it in the search square. What you are training now is to search and that searching is fun.

If your dog gets tired or weary, make the searches shorter and repeat only once or twice.

Take a Break

Stage 2. The search pattern

At this stage it is important not to be in a hurry and not to take short cuts in planning. If you are to successfully train your dog to be reliable in searching straight ahead, there must be no "accidents" where she finds something to one of the sides. Therefore it is better for you to take some time between each search. Quality takes precedence over quantity!

🐾 Carry on with the pattern of pathways as you did in stage 1 and continue to use fun objects.

🐾 Tie your dog or hold her whilst the helper goes out with an object.

🐾 Once the dog is confident to work at 30 metres, increase the distance, rewarding your dog for searching and finding each time. Normally building up the distance in increments of 5 metres is acceptable. Most dogs will understand the new distance by the time they have done between 2 - 5 repetitions. If five metres is too large a step, make the steps shorter – try three, two or even one metre. What is important is that you always make it a little more difficult, but not so difficult that your dog fails. Ensure that your dog has a fair chance of success. Remember that the feeling of mastering a challenge promotes learning.

☙ Continue to increase the length of the search. Even if you had to go down to increments of 1-2 metres initially, you should gradually increase the difficulty over time. When your dog runs out to 50 metres straight ahead of you, it is time to add the cue for this game.

1. Leave the dog and walk away from her in a zig-zag.

2. Place the object and return in a zig-zag.

3. Send the dog and praise when she returns.

3

Stage 3. Introducing the cue

I am always very particular about which words I use as a signal for my dogs to begin a set task, and even more careful about the time I choose to start introducing the words. Normally there are many things apart from our spoken words that may prompt our dogs to start working. In the case of the search square it may be the sight of either you or the helper going out to hide an object, and this is something to be avoided at all costs.

Before I introduce the verbal cue, I make sure that the dog has understood the game. I do not wish to give the dog the cue to complete the search square only to watch her run to the stream for a dip. A clever dog would be likely to learn that the cue for search square means "take a dip" in one to two repetitions! If you do it correctly though, it may be that your dog will learn what you want in one to two repetitions as well.

At this point you have completed stages 1 and 2, and your dog should be searching happily and reliably.

What you should do now is to repeat stage 2, except that in addition you let the dog do 2-3 searches in a row. The runs should not be long or

difficult at this stage, as the point where we introduce the cue is the second or third search. Prepare for success by choosing large objects highly valued by your dog.

When your dog searches perfectly twice in a row, the chances are that it will also be perfect the third time, which is when you introduce the cue.

Now prepare the third task.

🐾 The moment you release the dog, say "square" or another short and easily recognisable word that your dog will respond to and that will be unique to this game. The exact word you use is not really the point, but it must sound different from all other cues your dog has learnt, and you must say it the same way each time.

🐾 If you and your dog are successful this time, finish with a really good reward, play with the object and take a break.

After a short break, repeat the steps you just went through to teach your dog the cue. (If the dog failed, go back to stage 2, followed by stage 3 again.)

If the performance was a good one continue after the break by testing with search without giving the cue, before giving the cue at the second search.

Carry on in this way, verifying that the dog works by completing 1-3 searches with the given cue.

After 3-5 repetitions like this, your dog will have understood the cue; some dogs may understand it even sooner.

Anyway, it is high time for a major break! As always: stop when the dog completes the search square correctly and while she still wants more.

After the major break, you are ready to teach your dog to search when she does not see anybody going out to place any toys.

Stage 4. Searching without the dog having watched the preparations

You are still intending to make a scent pathway. The aim now is that the dog is no longer allowed to watch your helper placing the object. The dog should wait in the house, the car, or far enough away so that she cannot see or hear what is going on.

Walk in a zigzag as before and hide a favourite object.

Remember that whenever making something more difficult, the other parameters must be made easier if possible.

Train only one aspect at a time. This is why this search should not be long, and why the object should not be too difficult to find. You are just testing whether the dog will search without

having seen the task being prepared. Now you will find out if your cue means anything at all to your dog.

If the first "blind" search goes well, reward and take a short break. Then make a new search exactly like the previous. It is better to make too few than too many repetitions.

If it does not go well, go back to stage 2, followed by stage 3 before you make a new attempt at stage 4.

Stage 5. Searching without the scent pathway

At this stage, you and your dog should no longer be watching the preparation of the task. Now, you must also train your dog to search an area where there are no pathways of scent to help the search pattern. This may be the most critical phase in the training.

The first task to be completed without this scent pathway must be planned to lead to success. Initially it is best to place the object at such a distance that you know your dog will find it.

Some dogs rush out to 8-10 metres and start searching from there. So for dogs like these, this is where to place the object.

Other dogs might already start searching from 2-3 metres, and therefore this is your chosen spot. The aim is that the dog should learn that whenever you say "square" (or your chosen cue), there *is* something out there even if the scent pathway is missing.

Pick a large, interesting object in order to make it easy in the beginning.

As you have probably realised yourself, the real challenge is to place the object without creating scent pathways. If you are good at throwing, the problem is solved. Otherwise, use your imagination. There must not be a track leading to the object, so you will have to throw the objects to where they should remain.

Walk out parallel to where the search is supposed to be, and throw the object into the imaginary square. Or if you want the object placed at the far end of the "pathway", you can make a big curve around, coming in from the back to throw it.

If the object is placed too far away for the dog, she may start to search to the left or right before she gets to the object. If it is too close, the dog may run past it without noticing. If your dog has overrun the object, or has drifted too far to the sides without finding it, run sideways and call her. However, she should ideally be prevented from finding the object while she is running to the sides! But if she finds it anyway, you will just have to praise her and make a new (and better!) plan.

If all went well, praise, take a break and continue the training after a while.

If it didn't go so well, remember that *it was not the dog's fault* so there is no reason to be angry or disappointed with the dog!

Take a Break

Gradually move the object further away until the dog is able to reliably search the whole 50 metres, following the same steps you used in stage 2. This will usually only take a few sessions.

Remember the rule: there should be a maximum of five repetitions in a row.

When something goes wrong, always take time out to think! Why did it fail? Then, plan a new task and do what you can to eliminate any chance of error.

Two suggestions to help your dog succeed with the search square:

It may be an idea to lay the pathway up against the wind in order to let the dog get some help from it. If you choose the wind to help, don't do it too often, as the aim is for the dog to learn to search without any help from scent-pathways or wind.

You might like to try a larger object. Try an object that is big enough for the dog to notice when she approaches, but not so big that it is visible right from the beginning of the search. Grass and heather or other types of vegetation are good for this purpose.

Stage 6. Accuracy: learning to search from the first paw-step

I have no idea how many times I have heard proud dog owners claiming their dog is so good at the search square, able to cover the field perfectly and picking out whatever kind of objects have been placed, familiar or strange ones. Whenever I have had the chance, I have tested them!

Whilst the dog owner is busy preparing and not paying attention to me, I have dropped my Leatherman tool (in a leather cover) just a short distance (20 – 30 centimetres) inside the boundary of the square. No dog has so far solved this task. What about your dog? Do you think she would find it? Maybe I am too influenced by the seriousness of the search for land mines? No, I don't think so. The entire square should be searched, and the square starts at the imaginary line between the corner markers.

🐾 To teach your dog to begin searching from her first step, start from where your dog normally begins her real search (not the part where she runs out, but the part where she puts her nose to the ground). Most dogs have a pattern here: some rush out to 3, 10, 30 or even 50 metres before nose and brain are connected. Never mind where your dog starts to search, this is where you begin.

🐾 Let's say that your dog's habit is to rush out to 20 metres before beginning the search. Ok, then place an object at 20 metres and pay for the find.

🐾 Next time place it at 18 metres, and give a jackpot for the find.

🐾 The third time, place the object at 16 metres.

🐾 Carry on like this, until your dog starts to search from the very first step. You may have to shorten the first 4-5 metres after the starting point by only ½ metre.

🐾 Place the object closer and closer to the starting line, until your dog can find objects laying 20 cm from your feet. Now you can be proud that your dog is searching from the very beginning!

🐾 I recommend working in high grass or heather and using a rather large (and interesting!) object. If you only have short grass available, pick a small object of high value. The aim is that the object should not be visible as your dog is supposed to sniff to find it.

🐾 Once your dog can find an object from the very beginning, start to vary where the object is placed. Always remember to place the object within the imaginary pathway of scent that is 3-4 metres wide.

🐾 Each time your dog seems to have difficulty finding objects at a certain distance, train for this by starting at the point of success and gradually coming closer to the site at which the difficulty is experienced.

Stage 7. Introducing blank searches

You have very nearly achieved your aim!

However, until now your dog has probably found something every time, except for the few times she may have passed by the object and failed the task. So she is not totally unused to runs where there is nothing to find. Nevertheless it is necessary to put blank runs into the equation (a run where nothing has been hidden), to make sure your dog has the confidence to continue working even when it takes a long time before she finds anything.

To make sure your dog does not run sideways and thus find the object she was supposed to find later, you have to plan and prepare. A good idea is to place in advance the object that is to be found on the second run, using a recognisable point such as a path or a road.

🐾 First, send your dog out searching in a direction where you know there is no object. When the dog reaches 50 metres, praise her and call her back.

🐾 Immediately move a few steps to the starting point of the run where you hid something earlier, and send your dog out searching for it. Celebrate when she finds the object!

Using the wind

Another variation may be that you use the wind:

☙ Place an object and walk sideways towards the wind so that no wind can bring scent from the object to your starting point. To be absolutely sure, walk as many metres away as you need to in order to ensure that the dog will not find the hidden object before you want her to.

☙ Send the dog to search, praise her when she reaches 50 metres, and call her to you.

☙ Move directly to the spot that represents the starting point of the next search (where an object is hidden), and send your dog out searching. Share the moment when the dog finds the object. If she does not find it, send her out once again.

Each time your dog has searched an area where nothing was to be found, she must have a series of successful searches where she does find an object: at least 4-5 searches, and maybe even as many as 10 times. Then it is time once again to make a new blank search.

☙ Send the dog out on a search where there is nothing, praise her when she is at 50 metres and call her.

☙ Now move to a new spot where there is still nothing, and send the dog out searching again. Praise her while she is searching, and call her back once she reaches 50 metres.

☙ On the third search there must be an object of particular value to the dog. It should be placed so that the dog does not find it before the third search. Using the wind as I described in step 5 may be useful now.

Each time your dog has completed one or more blank runs, she must have a series of successful runs in order to keep her confident that there really are things to find.

Follow this recipe in gradually building up the number of blank runs until your dog can do at least 4-5 runs without finding anything and without losing her motivation.

Whenever you increase the amount of blank runs ensure that the task does not just become more difficult. When your dog has made three blank runs, give her a series of runs that are always successful, then one blank run and follow that by a new series of successful finds. Vary the runs in this way continually. Your dog should not be able to guess (or learn!) how many blank runs there will be; she must always believe there will be an object to find every time you, tell her to search.

Watch carefully that you do not establish any pattern in how many successful finds and how many blank runs your dog has: keep a training diary to help plan for success.

Stage 8. Generalisation

This will ensure that you teach your dog to search on all types of ground, in all kinds of environment and in all kinds of weather.

You are on the verge of having a dog that is fully trained to the search square now. The only thing remaining is to build up the dog's experience and motivation in working all types of terrain. Many have learnt that their dog does not perform in competitions because the dog does not recognise that type of landscape.

For a dog that is only used to one type of search square, the one in grass is quite different from the search square in heather. Therefore, make every effort to vary the training area at any possible occasion. As soon as your dog masters one type of terrain, move to another type. Never fail to lower your expectations when you change environment. Regard this as a totally new task - which is what your dog regards it as!

Having been presented with many types of environment, your dog will start to generalise and you will see that she needs less time to adjust to each new environment.

Train in the woods, the park, the school yard, the beach or the river bank. Have you trained on grassy fields with both livestock and their droppings present? Well, if not, train there too, but keep the dog on a long lead in order to risk no mishaps...

The weather is another factor that many dog handlers ignore. How easy is it to skip the training in bad weather? The result of not being trained in bad weather is either that your dog will not cope at all, or that her performance will be poorer than normal. And we claim that it is the dog who dislikes the weather!

Many years ago I did an experiment. At that time I had a Belgian Shepherd (Tervueren) who was a certified search & rescue dog in the Norwegian Association of Avalanche Dogs. Dirham was his name and he loved working in the rain! He enjoyed it so much because whenever it rained I would take treats and toys out into the forest to train tracking or the search square. This was because I wanted to make a conscious effort to see what effect it would have – and it worked! He became totally uninfluenced by bad weather throughout his entire short life, and if at any point he was influenced by the rain, he was rather more motivated than less. Just try it yourself.

Some final advice and hints

High motivation, or high stress?
Many dogs become very excited by watching the helper run and hide the object. An excited dog is a stressed dog. The more excited they are, the less thoughtful their work. As their concentration wanes, they become more liable to make a mistake. This is why my aim is to get away from the motivation of vision as soon as possible. For some dogs it may be necessary to remove the possibility of viewing the hiding of the object even earlier than I have suggested. In any case the helper should always make only a minimum of movements with the object to avoid catching the dog's attention. The aim of the game is to have a dog working thoroughly, quickly, and with concentration and focus. A dog with a high stress level may run quickly but will have a low level of concentration, and will have difficulties in responding to you. And last but not least, an over excited dog will have problems remembering what she is actually supposed to search for whilst running. Far too many handlers mistake high stress for high motivation.

Tests show that a panting dog is not really able to analyse scent (once the mouth is open), so this is one more reason for you to ensure you keep your dog calm.

If you have a dog that is easily aroused, you may have to change the stages so that stage 4 becomes stage 2. Then follow the stages in the original order. This way you can eliminate the strong motivation that may arise in the dog in watching the helper running away with the object. High motivation is not indicative of a lot of screaming and whining from the dog.

Giving back objects
Some handlers struggle to train the dogs to give objects nicely to the hand. Remember that this is

a detail you should train separately. Train it at home, in the club, in fact anywhere before you start to use it in the search square. Vary the objects: some large, some small, heavy, light, hard, soft and so on, including some that are more interesting for the dog than others. Watch that the payment the dog gets is always worth at least as much if not more than the object she gives you! When you are satisfied with the way she gives you the object(s) in other circumstances, you can also start to expect this in the search square. But then this is what you focus the training on, and nothing else. Place the object not too far away and ensure it is not too difficult to find, having a real jackpot available for the dog giving it nicely and correctly to you. Before the search starts it may even be a good idea to warm up with training the dog to give some objects to you.

Desire for objects

This is yet another thing you should train in a number of places other than in the square. In the square place only objects you know your dog likes and will retrieve happily. Train the love of objects in your house, garden, park, forest and in a number of other varied places. Collect objects of all kinds (even rubbish), always taking care to vary what you use. Objects may be items such as

a plastic bottle, a match box, a container for a roll of film, a button, a piece of fabric, cellophane, a pen, a tea spoon, a burnt match, a piece of cable, a plastic cup, a sock: anything of this kind as long as is not harmful to the dog.

Lay an object on the floor, and when your dog shows interest, praise immediately. You may need to hold it in your hand initially, before placing it on the floor. Gradually increase the distance between dog and object whilst expecting more and more interest before you praise. Look up the steps for this in the chapter on retrieve.

The dog's dependency on assistance

If you rely for too long a time upon visual motivation as assistance for your dog, you may run the risk of her becoming dependent on such support. If so, it is better that you occasionally test out how the game works without any help. If the dog is unsuccessful, just revert to using a little help once more. If your dog is successful, you don't need this help anymore.

Just as with the vision, help from the wind is a support the dog may become dependent upon. Use the wind direction rarely and always test that the dog can be successful without any help at all from the wind. If you face your dog towards the

Eventually you will get to the point where you can do a complete search. Here you can send the dog out to find a number of items one at a time. What a clever dog!

wind direction too often, she will expect this kind of help and will develop difficulties in going out to search unless she smells the scent of objects brought by the wind. During the training I recommend that you frequently give little tests to see what the dog can do without help. Stagnation on one level is just as harmful for the training as attempting to progress too quickly.

Just occasionally you can use searching against the wind as an extra motivation for your dog, but do so with caution: in search training use all help for your dog sparingly.

The finished search square (or the competition if you like)

Once your dog is fully trained you may decide to use the search square for having fun with your dog, or you may enter competitions or take part in a search and rescue operation. In all of these scenarios, I find it perfectly acceptable that your dog reacts to the airborne scent from an object and selects it from any direction. Only in training do I focus so much upon controlled searches straight ahead of me. If you regard any competition as a test that the system works, the cooperation between you and your dog will start to work as you would like it to.

If you do not go to competitions, I would recommend that you frequently, yet irregularly, set up an entire search with hidden objects as a test that the training is effective. It would be even better if you get another person to set up the square for you, so that you do not know where the objects are hidden. By doing this you will see whether you really can get your dog to cover the whole field, if she searches all the way and if she will use the wind as a helper for example. Note every deviation, select things to improve, and train these selective details until the next test. Of course, you must also take note of those points with which you are satisfied!

Allow your dog to search freely in the square if she chooses to. You can always call her and send her straight out if necessary. Dogs have the ability to search systematically without us training them. In addition you have trained your dog to work in a particular system when you want to. With these two search systems in use, you and your dog will

cover a field efficiently. Now you will see how pleased, contented and satisfied your dog is after having searched and found things for you.

After each complete square field searched I recommend many planned systematic searches where you take over control again.

Tacu, the dog that rescued our training area

During my time as a dog handler in the Association of Norwegian Search & Rescue Dogs, we had a little team working well together with several certified dogs. One of our most frequently used training areas was in a strip of wood owned by the government. During the moose hunting season, a team of hunters were obviously unhappy with us using the same area as they were, even though we normally did not use the area at exactly the same time.[1] Whilst we were considering whether we should change to another training area for a period of time, we were saved by one of the dogs. Tacu Rottweiler was out searching, and when he returned to his owner he was carrying a VHF radio in his mouth.[2] He had apparently found it whilst searching for hidden persons, and chosen to bring it back to Dad in case there was a treat to earn! The radio was totally undamaged and fully functional. Tacu's owner searched for the hunting team and told them what had happened. Of course, having got their radio back, they found it perfectly acceptable that we should continue to train there...

1 The right of access in Norway gives anyone the right to walk on meadows, fields, forest etc.

2 As this is some years ago, a radio like that represented a large amount of money – a month's salary for some!

Chapter 8

Finding lost objects

You return to the car after a walk in the park. Both you and your dog are tired and satisfied. When you go to unlock the car door, you realise that your keys are missing. It is already dusk, and of course it is too far to consider walking home. So, what now?

No problem, you just tell your dog to go and find the keys, and so she does. Three minutes later she returns with your keys in her mouth and a happy grin on her face. Great, isn't it? This particular dog may carry the keys in her mouth and return to you with them, but another dog could equally well find the keys and bark to get you to come and see what she has found. Both solutions may be perfectly satisfactory, and for dogs that do not enjoy carrying things in their mouth, barking is a nice way of telling you that the keys have been found.

Your dog can learn this with no great effort, and it is an amusing trick. Once fully trained your dog will be able to impress your friends by picking out your car keys from any number of keys in the same spot. Want to try? Read carefully:

Stage 1

Aim: to establish in your dog a strong interest for car keys.

Step 1 Start by holding your keys in front of your dog. Immediately she sniffs them, praise and give a treat. Make sure you hide the keys behind your back between each sniff.

Repeat 1-5 times, then take a short break

Step 2 Continue praising and treating for sniffing the keys, gradually holding them closer to the ground each time the dog sniffs them.

Repeat 1-5 times.

Step 3 If not before, this is the time to place the keys on the ground. Once your dog sniffs them, give lots of praise and toss a treat to the dog with the aim of making her move away from the keys. This is an exciting moment: wait and see if your dog returns to the keys by herself. Say nothing, just wait.

If your dog goes back to the keys, give her a jackpot (see page 12) and take a break.

If your dog shows no more interest in the keys, stop the training and take a break.

Take a Break

After the break, start at step one again, repeating all the steps. If she doesn't return to the keys as before maybe you should change to better treats!

Repeat this step until your dog happily runs (or walks) to the keys.

Repeat this first step until your dog readily goes to your keys. Each time your dog makes a mistake, give her a new chance to get it right. Make sure you always end with something successful. It is better to stop the training too early than too late. You can never make too few repetitions, but it is very easy to make too many...

Stage 2

Aim: to teach the dog what to do when she finds your keys.

Would you like your dog to retrieve your keys, mark them with her paw, or should she bark until you come and see? You may either decide this yourself, or wait and see what your dog prefers. Many dogs start to retrieve by themselves during this training.

Step 1 At this stage, you start to delay your praise for sniffing the keys.

☻ This time, once your dog has gone to the keys, wait maybe half a second, then longer and longer at each successive time. Often you will see what your dog will do to make you react and deliver a treat. Some dogs will start to paw the keys, for example. Whichever behaviour you are happy with, praise when your dog does it.

☻ Repeat a maximum of 5 times. When your dog offers a behaviour that you find satisfactory, for example a pawing, go to the next step.

Step 2 – Teaching the retrieve

If you wish your dog to retrieve, go even further. Withhold your praise longer and longer, allowing the dog to play roughly with the keys, using her paw or whatever. Watch carefully: whenever she has her mouth close to the keys, praise and treat. Gradually the idea will pop into her mind that it is her nose and not her paw that counts.

Step 3

☻ Continue watching the dog's nose: if she opens her mouth in the vicinity of the keys, give a jackpot! Some dogs do this more easily than others. If you are fortunate enough that your dog just picks the keys up by herself, you have achieved your aim and you can progress to the next stage.

☻ If not, carry on delaying the praise and be prepared for your dog to mouth at the keys. Be patient. Repeat in sessions of 1-5 repetitions, until your dog grabs and lifts the keys.

What is happening here is that the dog's frustration is growing as she realises that you are not praising her in the same manner as she is used to. When frustration increases, so does activity. However, if you wait too long, the dog will lose her interest totally, and walk away from the whole key project. This balance between keeping up the interest and withholding the praise hoping to get more action is both difficult and important. If you wait so long that your dog loses interest in the keys, go back to the very beginning (of stage one) and go through all the stages and steps once again. No harm done, it just takes more time.

Stage 3

Aim: to teach your dog that it is only your keys that she should be interested in and no-one else's.

Now you need someone to help you. As your dog should learn to seek out only your keys, this means that you should not touch the other keys you want to train with. Once you touch any other keys, they will smell of you and the difference between your keys and the others will be less clear for your dog.

Step 1

☻ Place your keys on the ground and get your helper to place one other set of keys nearby, between half to one metre apart, so the dog can see both sets of keys. Place the keys carefully so as to ensure that your dog will reach your keys first.

☻ Be quick to praise for sniffing your keys. Praise must come before she has time to leave them and go sniffing at the other set of keys.

☻ If your dog chooses the wrong keys, ignore this and start on a new task reducing the opportunity for your dog to make a mistake.

☻ If you still have no success, go back to stage 2.

☻ Repeat this 1-5 times, ensuring that, as always, you end with the best you can expect.

Step 2

☻ Within a short space of time, start to vary the position of the keys: as a next step place them side-by-side. Gradually increase the degree of difficulty: the most difficult task being to place your keys so that your dog has to pass the "wrong" set of keys in order to get to your set.

☻ Do not cheat! You must change the position of the keys every time in order to avoid the dog simply rushing to the keys without sniffing. Still be careful not to touch the other keys.

☻ Repeat this until your dog readily picks out your keys and ignores the other set.

Step 3

- Repeat step 2 above, only this time you use three sets of keys. One set is yours, whilst the other two belong to your friends or training partners.

- Continue to ignore any mistakes, and ensure you praise, treat or play when your dog chooses correctly.

- Continue until your dog readily picks your keys from the three different sets.

Step 4

- Gradually increase the number of sets of keys the dog must choose between. You will probably notice that 6 keys are no more difficult than 3.

- What might be more difficult is to pick your set of keys from those of others in your family.

Step 5

When the number of keys is no longer difficult, vary the distance between the different keys.

Try having them gradually closer until they all lie in one pile so that your dog has to dig through them all to find yours!

Stage 4

Aim: to teach the dog to respond to a certain cue.

Your dog now has a way of telling you which object she has found and where. However, you also need a way of communicating to your dog, "Oops! I've lost my keys! Please would you help me find them?" This is where having a cue comes in.

So far, the keys have been placed whilst your dog has been watching. Without watching this or having a certain cue, your dog has no way of understanding when and where to search for keys. So, when stage three is completed, and only then, are you ready to name this behaviour.

Choose a word, a hand signal or another signal that has not been used for anything else before. Each search game (and every other trick) must have its own distinguishable cue. I simply say, "My key" and this works fine for me and my dog.

Feel free to pick whichever word you prefer.

Step 1

- Prepare a simple task as you did in stage 3. Immediately you release the dog to find the keys, calmly give the cue you have chosen. There is no need to repeat the cue.

- Repeat this exercise three to four times in a row and have a break.

After repeating this exercise a few times your dog will associate the cue you have been using (word or signals) with this game. The aim is that whenever you give the cue your dog promptly starts searching for your keys.

Step 2

- Test that the cue works: while your dog is not watching prepare a task. Make the task very simple so that your dog is guaranteed success. Give the cue and observe your dog's reaction. If she sets off to search, she will have understood the cue. If not, repeat step 1 a few more times before returning to step 2 to retest her.

You have now reached the aim of the key ring training. *Congratulations!*

However, if you want to expand to an even bigger search, see the instructions below:

Stage 5

Aim: to make this real search in addition to choosing the correct keys.

Step 1

- This is the time to place sets of keys out of sight so that your dog must search for them. The first time go back to having only two sets of keys to choose from. (Maybe even only one!)

- Place the keys half a metre away, ensuring they cannot be seen by the dog.

Clever boy, Ajax!

How often do we underestimate our dogs' capabilities??

Ajax, a Swedish Bouvier des Flanders who was supposed to learn the trick about Mum's keys, had apparently understood long before the humans. He quickly learnt to go over to Mum's keys and bring them to her. When they came to the point where he should choose Mum's keys whilst ignoring the helper's keys, he resolutely picked the "wrong" keys, went straight to the keys' rightful owner with them, then went back to Mum's keys which he promptly picked up and presented to her.

☀ Give your dog an appropriate cue, watch carefully and praise once she sniffs your own keys.

☀ If it is too difficult for your dog, do this with only your own keys a few times before you get your friend to place his keys ready for the search.

☀ If it is still too difficult, go back to stage 3.

☀ If all goes well, repeat 1-5 times.

Step 2

☀ Increase the distance between the sets of keys.

☀ Place them out of sight for the dog, though still close enough for you to watch what is going on.

☀ Allow the dog to search without interruption.

☀ If your dog chooses the wrong set of keys, go back to stage 3.

☀ Praise whenever your dog reacts to your own keys.

☀ Repeat this until your dog readily searches and finds your own keys and either retrieves or marks them according to the training completed in stage 2.

Step 3

☀ As soon as your dog is searching and marking well with two sets of keys, gradually increase the number of sets (or other objects) hidden in the environment.

Step 4

☀ The last challenge is increasing the distance from the starting point out to where the sets of keys might be.

☀ Increase this gap gradually, until you have found a distance at which both you and your dog are happy. Whether it is 10 or 100 metres, it is just as good; it just depends on you and your dog and how you wish to work together.

It is important to be aware that you should only increase the difficulty of one factor at a time.

Either increase the distance to the sets of keys, the number of sets of keys, or the distance between all the sets of keys. It may be more difficult for the dog if she has to pass several sets of keys before finding the right ones. Out of sheer frustration, she may choose to retrieve the wrong keys just to find a solution. Make sure that you always stop the training before your dog is tired or excited, as this is when the likelihood for making mistakes is at its height.

When training with key rings, please note that their different appearance will also make a difference to the dog. Some have large, unusual fobs attached to the keys, while others are quite subtle. It may be a good idea to remove the biggest fobs from the key rings to prevent your dog from solving the task using vision.

Don't forget that dogs will always solve a problem the easiest way!

Only increase the difficulty of one factor at a time.

Chapter 9

The Lost Retrieve

Imagine having a dog that runs back the way you have just walked whether in the forest, field or elsewhere, and picks up whatever you have lost en route.

What an interesting way for busy dog owners of both exercising and stimulating your dogs! Your dog covers twice the distance simultaneously searching and working, yet she is doing something useful. It's a typical win-win situation, as far as I can see. The first few times you do this, you can use a toy or other object that your dog really loves. Later you can use anything, as long as you know your dog will retrieve it.

And it isn't even difficult. However, there is the premise that your dog must know how to retrieve.

What happens if your dog does not retrieve?

If she can't do this yet you might like to read chapter 8 stage 2 first. (page 47). Then return here once that task has been taught. Otherwise, you can still start the training of the lost retrieve, following the same stages, but substituting the toy for a chunk of some good food.

Ensure you offer the dog a suitably sized piece of food: for a Labrador-sized dog, half a hot dog will do. You could start the retrieve training in parallel if you wish, so that you eventually combine the two parts into the complete lost retrieve.

The first few times you train the lost retrieve, you can use a toy or other object that your dog really loves. Later you can use anything, as long as you know your dog will retrieve it.

Stage 1

Aim: to build up the dog's motivation.

Step 1

Pick a place with the minimum of distractions. Walk your dog on lead on a footpath. Stop in a peaceful area.

- Show your dog the toy and drop it on the ground whilst gently restraining your dog so she does not grab the toy before you are ready. Your dog is only allowed to look, but not touch!
- For you, the rule is that you can only hold or gently restrain the dog on the lead – NO pulling on your part! And under no circumstances can you say "no", "leave it", "don't touch" or anything like this. The object is not forbidden; you only want your dog to wait a little first.
- Invite the dog to follow you a few steps away from the toy, backwards in the direction from which you first came.
- After just 1-3 metres, whilst your dog is still focused on the toy, let the dog loose to go and fetch the toy.
- Time for celebrations! Finish by exchanging the toy with a delicious treat.

Notes.

However the dog chooses to deliver the item to you is unimportant. There should be no formalities, simply delight that the dog has found the toy.

Also, at this stage it does not matter whether your dog returns to you with the toy or not. The only important thing is that the dog enjoys finding the toy (or food!) If your dog runs away with the toy, take a break and read the chapter on retrieve. Or you may choose to train this exercise with food for a while.

The first few times that you release your dog, do not give any cue. Only when you know for certain that the dog will complete the first step do you give the cue.

Step 2

You can repeat step 1 after a few minutes' walk when the dog has been allowed to sniff, explore and relax.

- The toy should be hidden in your pocket. You should allow your dog to see that you drop the toy, and each time you do this you should walk a few metres (or steps) further back the way you came before allowing the dog to go to retrieve the toy.

Remember: after dropping the toy, you must always retrace your footsteps. In a way, your dog is back-tracking both her steps and yours.

☙ Repeat this 2-3 times in a row, then take a longer break for the dog to calm down and think about something else. To make sure the interest of your dog keeps high, always finish this training when she is at her most interested!

Take a Break

☙ You can repeat this exercise 4-5 times before going on to the next stage.

Stage 2
Aim: to teach the dog to find a hidden toy

You should continue to drop the toy whilst the dog is watching, but before releasing the dog walk back far enough to ensure that the dog cannot see the toy anymore.

☙ Increase the distance each time you repeat this game. How quickly you can increase the distance depends on your dog and how she works. Some dogs make rapid progress whilst others are slower. In terms of distance, this may vary from 20 – 50 metres according to the progress of the dog.

☙ Where the path is narrow, the object will often be hidden by heather or other vegetation. If you are on a road it may be wise to go past a curve before letting the dog loose to search.

Stage 3
Aim: to teach the dog to do this on a cue

Now your dog is searching successfully for the "lost retrieve" item without even seeing it and it is time to introduce the cue. "Lost" is the word I used to say in Norwegian.

☙ Pick a word that makes sense for you and that sounds different to any other cue your dog has learnt. The word should be clear and given in a friendly tone once your dog starts to move, simultaneously with her release to search for the toy.

☙ Repeat a few times to let the meaning of the word sink in.

☙ Repeat in series of 1-5 repetitions.

Stage 4
Aim: to test if the cue works

Until now, your dog has watched you drop the toy. To test if the cue really means something to the dog, you have to drop the toy without her seeing what you are doing.

☙ After secretly dropping the toy, walk back a few steps and give the cue.

☙ If your dog runs to get the toy, she has understood the cue.

☙ If not, you will have to repeat the previous stage a few more times before retesting.

☙ In the test phase you should only concentrate on the cue. The toy should lie quite close, but not so close that the dog can see it as soon as she turns her head. If she can see it after having run a few steps, that is fine.

Stage 5
Aim: to increase the length of the search

Only when you have tested that the cue really triggers your dog to work should you start on this stage. The idea here is to increase the distance back to where the toy is without the dog seeing that you are "losing" something.

If you train purposefully and regularly, your dog might even be able to run a kilometre back to fetch a sweet wrapper!

- As usual, plan the training so your dog is always successful.

- Carefully drop a favourite toy whilst your dog is occupied with something else.

- Turn around and walk back until the toy cannot be seen anymore.

- Turn yourself and the dog back towards the direction of the toy.

- Give the cue and release the dog.

You will have an idea of the distance your dog will run as this was tested in the fourth stage. It is best if the toy is placed just a little further away than the distance to which the dog is used to running. The point of this is that the dog should run a few metres, and just at the point where she is on the verge of giving up the toy should be visible.

- When you have done this a few times, your dog will run towards the toy with conviction when you give the cue.

- Repeat and increase the distance each time.

- Make a note of what you are doing and the point that you have reached! What you trained last is easily forgotten, and thus you risk stagnating at a certain level.

Even if you are not satisfied with how far your dog is going out, it is not a good idea to give the dog a cue for "forward" to help her to solve this task. This is not obedience training but a search game. If your dog does not go far enough when sent for a lost retrieve, it is either because the motivation is too low or because you are trying to push your dog too quickly. Your dog is not going out far enough simply because this task is not yet fully understood. Of course, in this case it is nonsense to start training something else.

Continue increasing the length gradually, until you think it is OK. Some people find 100 metres sufficient, others will only be happy with 1 kilometre. Even when your dog readily runs back 300 metres for the lost toy, give her also a short run every now and then as it is important that the task does not always increase in difficulty. Sometimes it should be easy in order for you to keep up your dog's motivation.

Stage 6

Aim: to teach the dog to deal with difficulties and distractions en route

Not all paths are straight, and some even have crossroads...

Your dog should learn to handle this. The dog has already tackled this kind of challenge after all (for example when you "lost" the toy), so a crossing should not be too complicated. Nevertheless the crossing of paths may be a challenge for the dog.

🐾 The first time the dog is required to search along a path where another path crosses, place the toy only ½ - 1 metre beyond the crossing, not more. You might like to choose a larger, more interesting toy in order to make it easier for the dog. The difficulty here is not to find the toy but to choose the correct direction at the crossroads.

🐾 When your dog has done this, increase the distance from the crossing to the spot where the toy is dropped.

🐾 After a few repetitions like this, a crossing will no longer present any real difficulty.

People as distractions

Another challenge for your dog may be meeting people or dogs en route. You might have chosen not to train for this, only teaching your dog this task in environments without distractions.

If you decide to start this training, you will find it may not be as complicated as you thought.

🐾 The first time your dog meets someone during the search, I recommend shortening the distance to the lost object so you can see what happens.

🐾 Choose an especially exciting toy.

🐾 The person the dog should meet must keep a good distance from the dog and should not try to make any kind of contact with your dog, not even eye contact. Do not choose someone who is your dog's favourite playmate!

🐾 If your dog approaches the person, the person must simply turn away from the dog and remain passive and boring. Carefully instruct

the helper beforehand, so you do not have to shout to each other.

🐾 Ideally the distance between the dog's route and the helper should be so far that the dog hardly notices the helper. In some cases the helper will have to stay 60 metres out in the woods or field to be sure that your dog will not be distracted.

🐾 When your dog easily achieves the task of finding the lost item with a person placed 50-60 metres away, start shortening the distance between the route and the helper. Eventually, your dog will run straight past a person coming up the path.

Should your dog be absolutely hooked on the helper, call your dog (remembering to praise her for coming!), and continue with a completely new session, making it slightly easier for you and your dog.

🐾 Make sure your dog has seen you dropping the toy; that the helper is far enough from the path that he is no distraction; and that the distance between the dog and the toy is short enough for the dog to complete the task. It may be a good idea, at least in the beginning, to pick helpers that do not have a particular relationship with your dog.

Good luck!

Dogs as distractions

• If you wish to train your dog to ignore other dogs en route, repeat the same formula as with humans.

• The dogs you use should be calm and not too attractive for your dog. The greater the interest you think your dog will have in the other dog, the greater the distance you need from the path to the other dog.

• Use toys of high value, and reinforce with really good treats when you have such a large temptation for your dog.

Stop immediately you have success. Don't be tempted to "try once more because it went so well", because this is when it most often goes wrong!

Argo searching amongst the cattle

Variations

Another variation of this game may be to "lose" more than one object on the same walk.

The first time you do this ensure you work at a short distance to allow you to watch what happens.

- On your way back from the walk carefully drop a favourite toy, walk 3-4 steps and then drop another toy. Your dog knows the game now, so she is not supposed to see this.

- Walk 5-6 metres more before sending your dog back for the toys.

- Praise and treat when she returns with the first one, and send her back immediately for the second toy. Praise and treat abundantly for finding toy number two!

- If your dog doesn't find toy number two repeat once more, but place the two toys closer to each other this time.

- When your dog has learnt that there may be more than one toy out there, start increasing the distance between them. The first may be 10 metres away; the final one could be 80 metres or even more.

- Remember as always to build up your training gradually in steps of two-three metres, continually increasing the distance between the objects as long as you want or as long as your dog enjoys the game. The first increments may be as short as only 2-3 metres, but more often you can increase the distance by increments of 10 metres as your dog becomes more experienced and realises that there really are several things to find out there!

Now you have a dog that runs hundreds of metres through the forest to fetch things you have lost. Not bad!

If you are hesitant to train your dog with items that are important or precious in case she cannot find them, then what? It can be rather annoying having to walk all the way back to pick up the ball, your glove or whatever you have "lost". Instead you could train your dog to retrieve any kind of waste! You can "lose" a piece of paper, a matchbox, a tiny leather tag or anything that doesn't matter if you never get it back. Just ensure it is not harmful to wildlife.

Chapter 10

Pancake Tracking

Your very first track!

Any dog can follow a track: it is an innate ability with which they are born.

Even so, it is still something we need to train. But why on earth should we do so? One reason is to work on the cooperation between dog and handler, and further reasons are covered in the chapter on tracking.

The most amusing part of a puppy class is when we have a tracking day. Puppies from the age of 10-12 weeks jump happily and purposefully through the heather to find out what happened to that pancake.

"Pancake?" did I hear you ask? Exactly! Pancake is what I wrote! (Or perhaps a hot dog!)

The very first track for a dog, young or old, will normally be made as a pulling-on-a-rope-track. I tie a pancake, a hot dog, a lamb chop or something else equally delicious to a piece of string or rope and pull it behind me where I walk.

The point of this is that instead of watching the person walking away, the dog becomes focused on what is jumping and bumping across the ground. At the same time, this item that is rapidly disappearing is something the dog really wants. By working in this way, I achieve something rare in dog training: killing two birds with one stone.

Pancake tracking step by step

You will need a stack of pancakes or alternatively a pile of hot dogs. Waffles may also be considered. In addition, you need a string or rope of 2-3 metres. For the dog, a comfortable flat harness and a long tracking line are necessary. Young puppies can do this just as well off lead. You may also find a helper useful, someone who can drag the pancake through the woods for you.

Step 1

* Check on the wind direction before you start: it is essential that if there is even the slightest breeze, the track should be laid with the wind at the back of the person laying the track.

* In addition to checking the wind, you must pick a spot where the track layer can disappear from the sight of the dog after a maximum of ten metres, preferably a shorter

distance, either by hiding in the vegetation, or by walking over or around a little mound for example.

* Tie the pancake to the string and give it to the helper.

* Put the harness and the long line on your dog, and hold the line.

* The helper should show the pancake to your dog by putting it on the ground and pulling the string a little to make the pancake move. Let the dog almost catch the pancake. Play cat and mouse for a short while, but be careful to avoid the whole pancake ending up in the dog's tummy right away! This does happen now and then, which is why you should have a stack of pancakes with you. If the dog manages to have a nibble of the pancake, this is perfect!

* Next, the helper goes out into the woods pulling the pancake behind with the dog being able to watch. Your job as the dog handler is nothing but gently holding the dog back at this point.

🐾 Allow the dog to take two-three dog steps forward in the direction of the pancake. Do not give your dog any commands or cues, absolutely no "sit", "calm", "wait" or anything. If you attempt to encourage your dog by giving exciting little shouts or whispers, you only risk distracting the dog from the pancake and diverting the attention to yourself. It is better to remain passive and calm and allow your dog to peep in the direction of the pancake that is disappearing.

The helper's task.

🐾 The helper walks into the woods and disappears. The helper walks into the woods trailing the pancake. Once out of sight of the dog, or after a maximum of 10 metres, the helper should pick up the pancake. The pancake should not be pulled all the way, as the dog should be searching for humans rather than pancakes.

Whilst dog and handler wait for the helper to lay the track, the dog will be likely to wander around a little, perhaps sniffing the path you are on. Allow this, but do not begin to talk to the dog, pet her, play or give commands. It is essential that you remain passive during the waiting time, and restrain yourself from giving any encouragement or other distraction. Each time the dog returns to the beginning of the track, allow her to move forward a metre or two by letting the line slide through your hands, as payment for remembering where the track is.

You should repeat this every time your dog has left the track and returned to it by herself. Keep hold of the line all the time so the dog cannot go any distance away from the track. You should say nothing to your dog, neither give praise nor a cue.

Once the helper is hidden, allow the dog to follow the track. The first few times you do this, you should not give a cue to the dog. Simply follow behind and gently hold the line allowing it to slide through your hand, ensuring that the end of the line does not slip through your fingers. The dog can walk 4-5 metres in front of you in order to allow her to work without you stepping on her heels. Keep a normal walking pace, do not run! If you think your dog is too fast, slow her down

gently by holding a little more firmly on the line. If the dog happens to lose the track and you get totally lost, it is better to interrupt the exercise and walk back to make a new track shortly afterwards.

Some dogs like to drift off to the sides all the time instead of following the track accurately. Allow your dog to do this, but you should slow down, stop and hold the line gently until your dog starts to sniff and follow the track again. As soon as you believe the dog is back on track, follow her. Whilst your dog is sniffing and checking up other things, always stand still. Most dogs will become more accurate with experience.

When your dog finds the person with the pancake, join in the celebrations: praise her and tell her how wonderful she is. You might even have some extra pancake in your pocket...

If your dog does not find her way, something which occasionally happens, you should think about what may have gone wrong. Was the track too long? Was the vegetation too high?

If your dog did not dare to cross the stream, perhaps there are too many distractions around. Or perhaps she was tired or recently had a large meal. If any one of these is the case, change whatever needs to be changed, and give it another try. Always move to a new spot when you lay a new track, to avoid the new track from crossing and being confused with the first one.

Whatever you do, do not help your dog to find the pancake. If you do, the dog will learn to rely upon you rather than herself, and you will not be able to make any more progress. All you need to do is to make a new track every time something goes wrong. No harm done.

Just occasionally, a dog may not dare to or want to follow a track made by someone she doesn't know. If this is the case, I let the owner take the role of the helper and disappear into the vegetation with a pancake on some string, whilst either I hold the dog, or else someone that she is not frightened of holds her.

Now the owner waits in the forest with the pancake, and a few minutes after the owner's disappearance the dog will follow whilst the helper holds the line. In some cases it is sufficient to do it like this just once; for other dogs you will have to give them several opportunities to track the owner before the dog eventually wants to follow the track of someone unknown. Over time dogs build up self-confidence and motivation, and then they will be able to track any stranger.

If you would prefer to work without a helper, you will have to tie the dog to a tree, and then play the helper's part by disappearing with a pancake on a piece of string. Leave the pancake with some of your property (t-shirt, bag etc) as a jackpot for your dog.

Once you are back with your dog you should act as the handler again, and, without hesitation, allow your dog to follow the track. Most dogs will be more curious about following their owner's track than that of a stranger. NB: It is essential that you only do this if your dog is safe and calm when you leave it alone.

Step 2

A dog that has successfully completed between one to three tracks of this nature should now be given more challenging tasks.

There is a choice between two ways of progressing: you can either lengthen the track, or once it has been laid, you can lengthen the amount of time that passes before the dog is allowed to follow it. However, it is important that you do not increase both difficulties at the same time.

During this step we move from laying a pancake track where the dog watches to laying a track where the dog cannot see what is happening.

Once your dog has done a few tracks as described in step 1, she will start to understand what you are aiming at. At this point it is time to move away from allowing her to watch the track-laying in order to take away the impact of vision.

The easiest way to test your dog's interest in tracking is to make a short track of some 20-30 metres out of her view. The track should start from a path or road so that you can easily access it and also remember where it is. It is a good idea to mark the spot by either digging a furrow in the ground with your foot, or hanging up a ribbon to mark the spot.

Your dog should be wearing a harness attached to a long line. Start a few metres away from where the track is, and simply walk towards the beginning of the track letting your dog sniff. Your dog should ideally be in front of you. When your dog arrives at the track, she will probably follow it, and you should immediately follow her. At this stage it is important that the dog finds the reward very quickly, and this is why the track should be short, a maximum of 30 metres.

If your dog does not want to follow the track without having first seen a pancake disappear,

make a so-called "double task" to help her remember what this is all about.

The tracklayer should make a short track and leave some personal property along with a pancake or some other goodies at the end. The dog must not see this. Mark thoroughly where the track begins either with ribbons or by making indentations on the ground. Once the track is made, the helper should return to you and your dog. Make a new pancake-pulling-track (by the same person) on the other side of the path, and let the dog do the track as usual. After having found the pancake and received a lot of praise, you walk directly to the beginning of what is now the "old" track. Allow your dog to sniff and check it out by herself. Do not say anything or try to help your dog in any way, as this will normally only disturb her concentration. Most dogs will pick up this track. If this isn't the case, lay a few more "pulling pancake tracks" before giving your dog another opportunity to pick up a track she has not seen being laid.

Glenshee's first tracks

My little Scottish deerhound was presented to his first track at the age of 4 months. We were in the forest, he, Troll and I. Glenshee and Troll waited by a tree whilst I pulled a colourful pencil case full of chicken a little way through the woods. Glenshee tried to catch the pencil case as well as he could, and waited impatiently until he was allowed to pick up the track. The first time he was quite unsure and hesitant, but found the pencil case full of chicken after only 30 metres! He was presented with a new track immediately after, and this time he followed with confidence and determination along the track straight to the chicken fiesta!

Chapter 11
Tracking

Tracking

This is where dogs track us down by following our exact footsteps.

On a walk with your dog and family, you might have seen your dog following tracks without really noticing or even really thinking about it. If a member of the group leaves the path for a reason and returns, the dog will often check the route to see what that dog or person explored during this escapade. Even a dog that is kept on lead when someone goes behind a bush will run out to check the track when let off lead again. Dogs are naturally curious and are naturally talented at tracking.

If your dog is a puppy or is totally inexperienced in tracking, I would recommend that you start with the chapter about pancake tracking. This would take between one to three days, and then you can return to this point again.

A track is the impact on the ground made by something or somebody moving. This is the simple short explanation. Anything that moves leaves a track, whether it be a person, a tractor, a bike, a moose, a mouse or an insect.

Have you noticed that you can smell the scent of perfume when a person passes you on the street? When a person has been in a room, we can sometimes smell their scent even after that person has left the room. The scent literally "sticks" to the environment.

So, what exactly is a track? What makes it possible for the dogs to follow a track? We certainly know that they can do so; just think of hunting dogs finding game, for example.

When someone moves through the terrain, they make an impact on the ground. Not all imprints are visible for our eyes, but they are still there. Vegetation is crushed, insects and other small creatures are killed or injured and the ground itself is compressed so that little pockets under the ground are squeezed and any gases or fermenting liquids present leak out. Even our

human noses can smell broken vegetation. When I step in a boggy area, even I can detect the smell of the gases that evaporate. Usually, of course, we do not smell anything from our own footsteps.

But the dogs do.

The tracks our dogs can smell, have three main components:

Broken and disturbed ground

On a fresh track (normally meaning up to two hours old) the smell of disturbed ground is strong. It will be at its peak after 15-20 minutes, and then decrease over time as the "wounds" heal. The wounds on the plants will heal, the dead insects will be eaten, will rot or will dry out, and the stream of gas that oozes out of the squeezed pockets will die away. Nevertheless, this is what catches the dog's interest initially. It is only later that the dog learns to sniff for the scent of the species.

Scent of the species

Also incorporated into the track is information about whichever species has moved in the immediate vicinity, whether it be human, bird or dog. The scent of the species consists simply of molecules that fall off as we move. Hair and dandruff and molecules from our body and

clothes fall from our bodies onto the track. When tracking wild animals, one often finds faeces and urine along the way. Injured animals may also leave blood stains. Dogs can "read" from the track no matter what has passed that way: moose, hare, human beings or even a wheel chair.

Scent of the individual

Each individual has its own unique smell, similar to finger prints. In addition to knowing that the track was laid by a dog, your dog has the ability to read which dog left the track. Information like age, sex, sexual status (such as if a bitch on heat has passed by), and whether or not the dog was healthy are just a few examples.

It is wise to have this knowledge in mind whilst laying tracks. There is, for example, no such thing as an area with absolutely no tracks. Someone has moved there at some time. It may have been a person, an animal or a vehicle of some kind. Then you come and lay your track on top of this, believing that "your" track is the only one there.

But now you know. At least you have an idea about how much information lies on the ground, and hopefully as a result you will show more patience when a novice dog needs some time to check it all out and to take in all the information.

In addition, when you memorise how dogs prioritise the use of their senses, you will have a good chance of succeeding in creating a good tracking training programme for you and your dog.

Equipment

As I have seen to what extent unsuitable equipment can ruin an otherwise good training session, I will give some advice on equipment.

Imagine having laid a long and well-prepared track for your dog. The dog starts off perfectly, tracking beautifully. Then your dog loses the track whilst fighting her way through some heavy vegetation. The dog works hard to find the track again, but meanwhile the long lead has got completely stuck in the bushes. You have to sort out the lead and the dog and start all over again, hoping to find your way back to the same track. An inexperienced dog will easily lose her motivation in all this mess.

Tracking line

So, the most important piece of equipment is an 8-10 metre long line, preferably one that is stiff, that does not soak up water, that does not cling tight around trees or has a knot or loop in it.

The best lines are ones that are plain and smooth so they will not get stuck.

My tracking lead stems from 1988 and I guard it like treasure! It has never got stuck (touch wood), in contrast to the fate of most other leads I have seen used. Ask experienced people what they recommend, and test out for yourself what you prefer.

Harness

The tracking line should be attached to a comfortable harness, not the collar. Buy a simple harness that fits your dog well and one that does not hurt your dog anywhere. It is best to try a

number of different harnesses on your dog in order to find one that is an appropriate fit.

Before you go training, you must have something your dog wants to work for - some payment. It can be a favourite toy, hot dogs, liver, meaty bones, chicken, steak or cheese, for example. Ask your own dog what she prefers. Even if she loves her ball, it may be that she prefers something else (preferably edible) as payment for tracking. It is important for you to be aware of those things in order to take advantage of your dog's preferences in any future training. However, remember that preferences do change from day to day, so do not assume that your dog will always want chicken even if that is today's favourite.

Personally, I like to emulate as closely as possible what would happen during a wild dog's successful track: the dog will follow a track which could be long and wearying. At the end of this track the dog will catch, attack and kill the prey. Eventually, the dog will eat the prey on the spot. If the prey is killed in a safe place, the dog might even take a nap before eating more. To this end I choose a payment for my dog that will take some time and some effort to fetch and/or eat. It might be a pig's ear, some dried fish, a stuffed Kong or a big meaty bone, for example. For puppies and small dogs, an empty toilet roll with some food inside is a good prize. Use your imagination and come up with something that takes time to consume without being too difficult and discouraging.

Since most of our dogs are tracking people, it is a very good idea for a person to hide and hold the payment. In this case, the dog will not "kill" the track layer, but will regard this track as one leading to the reunion of the pack. I even bring a treat for myself, so that my dog and I can have a nice party together.

Motivation, trigger and payment

Imagine being invited to help your friend paint his house. To bribe everyone to come, he promises to take you all to the pub and pay for a nice meal. When the house is painted, he says there is no restaurant, but that take-away pizzas will arrive soon. Even if the pizza is delicious and you enjoy it, you have to admit that you feel that he has cheated on you, don't you?

This is exactly the same with dogs. If you bribe the dog using a ball, the ball must be payment for the task. In this case the ball appears as the promise, and it is cheating to pay your dog with treats or anything other than the ball.

If you tease the dog with a pancake during the initial track, this pancake is the trigger for tempting the dog to work. Finding the pancake along the track is the reward for a job well done, and is meant to increase the chances that the dog will follow a similar track another time.

If you want to build up the dog's motivation to go tracking with you or for you, it is essential to provide a solid connection between the trigger and the reward.

Be predictable and reliable. Keep your promises!

Tips for the assistant track layer

I have no intention of giving complete instructions for assistants here, but I want to give some advice in the hope that it will help you avoid the most common mistakes.

If, as an assistant, you are asked to lay a track for a training partner, make sure you get careful instructions about what is required. Likewise, if, as a dog handler, you ask someone to lay a track for

you, take the time to give specific information to your helper.

Have you ever noticed how difficult it is to keep a straight line when walking in the woods? Without a compass or using some simple tricks, it is almost impossible to achieve this.

What about making a turn at an angle? Usually, we mean a right angle, of 90°. Unfortunately you won't be able to do this accurately unless you know the tricks. Any right turn we take whilst walking in the woods is likely to be at an angle of more than 90°.

Bearing these two facts in mind, can you see how easy it is to get lost?

Imagine that you are about to lay a track that is supposed to be 300 metres forward, with an angle to the left followed by walking another 200 metres in a new direction, making another turn to the left at a specific angle again, walking a further 250 metres and placing the reward there. If you manage to follow the instructions carefully, you will end up about 200 metres from the spot from which you started. But sometimes it happens like this:

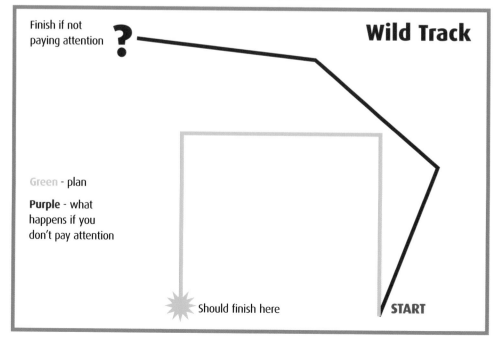

Finish if not paying attention **?**

Wild Track

Green - plan

Purple - what happens if you don't pay attention

Should finish here

START

Hints to help you keep your direction

If you don't want to use a compass, look around and pick out a tree, boulder or something that is easy to recognise and pinpoint this object as your exact direction. Find at least two, preferably three such landmarks and you will have a correct course that is easy to follow. When you reach the first landmark, make sure you look for a new one behind the last one so that you always have two or three marks in front of you.

In order to make a right angle, you will need three landmarks. One must be in the direction in which you are walking, one will be at the angle itself and the last one will be in the new direction. When you reach the point where you are to turn, turn to the direction you came from and double check all your landmarks to make sure that the angle will be correct. Again, pick three further landmarks in the new direction, and carry on walking.

Some advice on placing objects on the track

As a track layer, you will sometimes be asked to place objects on the track. These may be toys or other items, and you should lay or drop them on the ground between your feet, taking care never to throw them to the side. The point of this is that the dog should react to things a missing person may have dropped during his track. Objects should not usually be placed in the vicinity of an angle.

Place the object on the ground 20 metres before or after making an angle. Normally, there will be a particular object to be placed at the end of the track. This should be something the dog values highly, like a precious toy, or an extra tasty piece of food. On most occasions, you will be asked to sit there holding the food or toy, waiting for the dog to find you.

If you are not supposed to wait on the track, place the final reward on the ground and continue to walk in the same direction for another 5-10 metres before making a wide turn to get to wherever you want to go, either back to the dog and owner or to hide somewhere, being very careful not to cross your own track and mess it all up.

For some dogs it is not advisable for the track layer to return to the dog and owner as the dog is so intelligent that she will understand that the missing person is no longer lost. In her eyes there will be no problem to solve and consequently no reason for her to follow the track!

Ribbons

Normally I prefer not to use ribbons (generally made of crêpe paper) during the track. But in some circumstances where following a track is more difficult it may be very useful to do so. The drawback with using ribbons is that the handler often fails to learn to trust the dog and tends to rely on the ribbons as confirmation of being on the right track. When you have learnt to "read" your dog, it is easy to see whether the dog is on the track or not. Nevertheless, many people do like to use ribbons.

When you use ribbons to mark a track, place them so they hang high from a tree or bush, for example. They should be easy to see from a distance, and be hung high enough not to disturb the dog. The ribbons must be placed along the route you walk, so avoid taking little steps to the sides to place the ribbons.

The whole point of using ribbons is that they are supposed to be visible! This is why they should be quite long and carefully placed so that when standing next to a ribbon you should be able to see both the next one and the previous one.

The dog's reward

Now, let's examine our behaviour towards the dog. Whether experienced or not, most dogs will enjoy finding a human friend on a track from time to time, especially in their initial training. However, it is important to also give the dog the opportunity to find people in later stages of training. If you train for search and rescue, this is the whole point! For many dogs it is hugely satisfying to find somebody there.

If you volunteer to be "found" you are effectively the reward provider, and therefore it is essential that you know which reward is the dog's favourite. Does the dog prefer tug of war, cat & mouse play, treats or touch? If it is the latter, then you should know how the dog prefers to be touched and it is important to find this out from the dog before you lay the track. If you don't know the dog very well it is vital that you don't seem challenging or threatening. Bend your knees rather than leaning over a dog. Don't stare. Never touch a strange dog over or around the neck. You should neither hold a dog tightly nor be rough with any dog you do not know. Finding you is supposed to bring nothing but pleasure for the dog, certainly any sign of disapproval however slight is absolutely forbidden.

I hope that I have given you a broad outline of your task as a helper and track layer. You will have to experience the rest during training. Good luck, and enjoy your track laying.

Track training, step by step

After a few tracks using this method, your dog will have several experiences indicating that tracking is exciting and that something fun or very enjoyable will be waiting somewhere along the track. And you will have gained some experience of what is easy and what is not so easy for both you and your dog.

One rule I follow carefully when training dogs, is that I change only one parameter at a time. This means that only one thing should be made more difficult for each track. Imagine laying a track that is older and longer than before, and is also in a totally new environment. To your surprise, the dog fails to follow the track. In this case, you will not know whether it is the age, length or the new place that was the problem, and the training session has not really shown you anything useful. If this track was successful, be happy – you were lucky! Just remember next time to change only one thing at a time.

Now your dog has done a few tracks and will be capable of picking up and following a track without seeing a pancake or a person disappearing into the forest. This is the time to make it more challenging. But first you will have to choose how to make it more of a challenge. Should your initial step be to increase the length or the age of the track?

The answer to this is not always straightforward. Normally I increase the age of the track first, especially for very eager, quick dogs.

How old should tracks be?

How old does a track have to be before it is impossible for the dog to follow it?

Actually, I don't know. A student of mine, who trained her dog for injured game, reported that her Rottweiler could follow the blood track of a deer that was 125 hours old, a little more than 5 days! Impressive, isn't it? Others have mentioned one week, some even 1 month. Once I heard a story of a Bloodhound that could find a track that was one year old. Unfortunately this information has never been confirmed as fact.

A track of 15-20 minutes

The first tracks you and your dog have been following will be between 4-10 minutes old, as fresh as a daisy. As soon as your dog can follow a track without seeing a pancake being pulled, you can start to increase the time you wait before beginning the track. First you can wait 15-20 minutes before your dog is presented to the track. Most dogs can handle this easily, while others may find it more difficult. If it does not work, make a new track right away that is within the time you succeeded with before, and then take a break. Next time you have a training session, start with a short track of 5-10 minutes as a warm up, and then present your dog with a new track that is 5-10 minutes older than the first. Carry on like this until your dog easily follows a 20 minute-old track. If at any time your dog fails to complete a track, present one, two or three tracks that are

easy enough to be mastered before increasing the difficulty.

The next step is to increase the age of the track up to about 30-45 minutes. Increase the age in increments of 15 minutes, until the dog can successfully complete tracks that are an hour old. After this stage, you can increase the age in increments of 20-30 minutes.

Don't hesitate to stretch the boundaries a little: if it doesn't work, all you have to do is make a new track which is not so old, and again carry on increasing the age but now in smaller increments.

Even when your dog can follow tracks that are two hours old, you should give her fresher tracks now and then. Vary the tasks continually, and guard against stagnating a particular level.

How long should the tracks be?

As quickly as you increase the age of the track, you should also increase the length. Getting accustomed to 50 metre-long tracks is not our aim! Dogs can easily follow tracks of several hundred metres. I know dogs that have tracked continually for 3 to 5 hours over a distance of several kilometres.

For your dog, you can probably increase the length of the track in steps of 50 metres. If your dog can follow a 50 metre long track with you hanging on to the tracking line, the chances are that the same can be possible with a 100 metre long track as well. Continue increasing the tracks in 50 metre increments until at least 300 metres is "normal" for your dog.

After succeeding with a track of 300 metres, you can probably increase the distance in even greater increments, possibly even of 100 metres. If the track gets too long for your dog, follow the same rule: just make a new one that is shorter, and build it up in shorter increments. It is all a question of keeping up the motivation of your dog along with her physical condition.

Experiment with your dog and find a means of progress that works well and offers success. Sometimes you may have to increase the length by only 30 metres, at other times you can go straight from 300 metres to 500 metres. This very much depends on the weather and the motivation and experience of the dog. The golden rule is to always keep challenging a little, giving your dog gradually bigger challenges.

Most dogs enjoy those challenges.

Suggested progress

Personally, I prefer to work on increasing the age of the track, until the dog is easily coping with tracks that are one hour old. This gives me the room for flexibility, as the tracks now can be anything between 5 minutes and 1 hour old. By training once a week, you should be there within 2-4 weeks.

Working within the time frame of a track that is up to an hour old I start to make the tracks longer, until 300 metres can be achieved. So you have now succeeded with hour-old tracks that can be as much as 300 metres long. Quite good!

The next step is to work on the issue of time again for a while. You might increase the time until you succeed with tracks that are 2 or 3 hours old. After this, concentrate once more on the length. In this way you may have periods or single sessions focusing on various challenges all the time.

So, at what point do you stop giving yourself and your dog challenges, being satisfied with what you have achieved and feeling that you can do no more?

Think of it like this: without challenges, big or small, work easily gets monotonous and boring. There are challenges other than age and length...

Track crossing a path or stream

A challenge may be old tracks, long tracks, more difficult terrain, a track crossing a path, road or stream, a track through a barn, over a fence, along a fence... there are really so many possibilities. Just use your imagination.

The first time your dog's track crosses a path there is a greater degree of difficulty as the path contains so much scent which makes it easier (and more tempting?!) to follow the other path. Ask the track layer to take very short and shuffling steps whilst crossing the path and the first few metres after the path as well. It is also a good idea to place a little reward, like a small piece of food 5-6 metres after the path, to pay the dog for making the right choice in following the track and not the path. Think about what is the challenge in the track, and place the reward so that it counts (in the dog's opinion!) as payment for that particular challenge, and not for the track as a whole. This means that you can have several little payments en route on a single track.

Reproduce the described suggestion when laying tracks crossing a stream or other similar distractions.

Angled tracks

As human beings, we believe that working with angles in a track is difficult. This is why we tend to lay all tracks straight forward when we start the training of a tracking dog. After having done this a few times, the dog has learned that tracking together with us, means that it is literally straight ahead, and that the task does not need much concentration. For this reason, I always lay tracks in the shape of a J or a U or L right from the very beginning. Thus I eliminate the possibility of the dog finding the solution merely by rushing straight ahead.

Very early on, I introduce several arcs and turns in the track. By making sure I always vary the challenge there are fewer traps to fall into. The most amusing tracks follow someone who collects mushrooms or picks flowers: they may wander in one direction then in another, they may stand still for a while, walk a bit further, and it is rare that they keep going for long in the same direction.

If you have a dog that tracks at high speed, or that already has an established problem following turns, you may use ribbons to mark the turn. In this way you will have a chance to slow the dog down when approaching the turn. Watch the ribbons. If the dog wants to go the wrong way (be 100% sure now!), hold gently on the line (no jerks!). You should not say anything, whether it is "NO" or anything else. Leave it to your dog to find out what is necessary. Once your dog picks the right direction, let the line slide smoothly through your hand, and follow the dog. It is a good idea to give a large or small payment 8-10 metres after the turn. If it is too difficult for your dog, break off immediately, call your dog and praise her for coming to you. There is no reason to be (or show that you are) disappointed. The only way to progress is to lay a new (easy) track to keep the motivation, and then make a new task with a turn, maybe quite a wide angle at first, and then one that is more and more acute.

Tracks crossed by others

The term "crossed tracks" means that somebody has walked across the track after you have laid it. Thinking back to the dogs' priority of the senses, you will realise that the most tempting and logical thing for the dog to do is to follow the most recently laid track. This of course, is the one "on top" of the one you want your dog to follow. When I train a crossed track with dogs, I choose open terrain that is easy to survey, and in this case I will definitely use ribbons. The person laying the track uses red ribbons for example, and will make the track around 40-60 metres long, hanging visible ribbons all the way along it. After about 25-40 metres the track layer places two ribbons side by side, and carries on a further 10 –

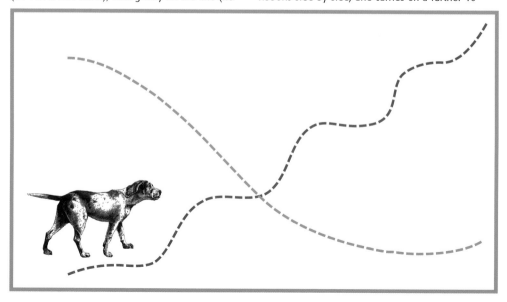

20 metres before placing the jackpot. Mark the jackpot spot with some extra ribbons.

Next, I ask another person to lay the crossing track. This person will use blue ribbons, and will start off 5-10 minutes later. His aim is to cross the original track exactly where the two ribbons are. All the way along, he should hang up blue ribbons, and where the blue track crosses the red track it is crucial that the blue ribbons can be seen very easily. Thus I have two very clearly marked tracks: a red one which the dog is supposed to follow, and a blue one which the dog should learn to ignore. When both track layers are back, dog and handler prepare to follow the track.

When the dog comes to the blue track, she is likely to check it out in both directions. This is natural, and you must allow her to do it. Simply hold the lead in order to restrict the dog from walking more than 3-4 metres in the "wrong" direction. Once she is back on the right track (the red one), you should continue to follow her.

This is a situation where the usage of ribbons is brilliant. After some metres following the right track, your dog will find the jackpot as payment for the correct choice. Join in with the celebrations and tell your dog how wonderful she is! Any dog that I have trained in this way has learned what to do within a few tracks, with some dogs learning the entire process in as few as 2-3 tracks.

Another variation, may be to make a longer track, 80 – 150 metres which is crossed by 2-3 tracks. The crossing tracks should have a distance between them of around 30 metres. Place a treat after each crossing to reward your dog for making the correct choice each time. Plan the crossings similar to those suggested above. Ideally, I use one colour for each track, meaning that you need 4 colours in this case.

Most dogs will check the first crossing quite thoroughly, a little less thoroughly on the second crossing, and very little on the third crossing. Dogs learn fast if we prepare the right tasks for them.

Teaching the dog to find where the track begins

Every so often, we do not know exactly where the track begins and only have a vague idea. In this case, the dog will have to find out by itself. So far we have brought our dogs directly to the starting point. To teach the dog to search for the track, I always begin by letting the dog find the track sideways, roughly at a 90° angle. The first time I begin no more than 10-20 centimetres from the track, the next time it's ½ metre, then 1 metre, then 2 metres etc, until the dog can work forward 5-10 metres searching for the track. If you are training for competitions or a particular search and rescue programme, check out the necessary requirements and train with

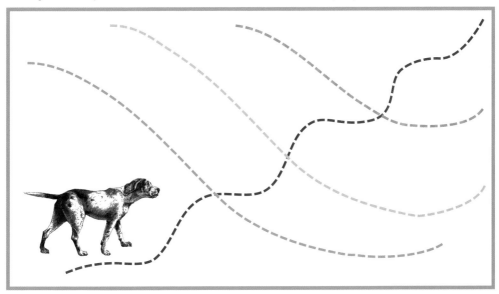

these criteria as your minimum aim of performance. If you train your dog with your organisation's demands as your maximum aim, you have no security blanket or margin of safety, and chances for failure are high.

Work sign, or cue

I dislike the word "command" when working with dogs. The English word "cue" is wonderful. Instead of sounding like a demand, it represents an invitation to cooperate and a permission to work.

Regardless of what we call it, I always wait before giving the cue until I am sure that the dog knows how to perform the task, and that the likelihood of performance is extremely high. When it comes to the tracking, I wait until the dog has tracked 2-5 times without any signal. Once the dog performs according to my expectations and starts tracking willingly, I introduce the cue "track" immediately before the dog starts to track. You may pick any word you like, but avoid the word "search" as most people will use that word for many other purposes as well. You need a different cue for different behaviours.

Various challenges

If you are a club member or if you are involved in any type of team training together, you will have some good opportunities to receive unusual challenges. Make it a habit in your team to occasionally invent surprising and entertaining tasks for each other that may additionally show new sides of the training, the dog or the handler...

If someone has a birthday, for example, you may decide to offer as a present a track where the objects along the way are little gifts like coins, bank notes or wrapped parcels, for example. Make sure that some gifts are for the dog, too.

Lay a track where the age of the track will change part way through. Send the track layer out with a book, a thermos flask and a sandwich. After a few hundred metres, he can sit down to read, eat and have his coffee. He might even sleep a little, and not until an hour or so has elapsed will he continue the track. The rest of the track may be 100 to 300 metres long, depending on the dog. What is interesting here is to see how (or if!) the dog has any reaction to the break and time change in the track.

Here is another idea that you will need to plan a couple of days in advance:

The track layer should arrive at an agreed spot where there is a bike. He should walk with the bike for the first 30-50 metres, then ride the bike for a stretch of around 50-100 metres and at the end of this point is a real welcome for the dog, including the track layer, the bike, a huge steak...

Track leading in the "wrong" direction

When you want to make a real challenge (as opposed to a trap) for a fellow dog trainer, lay a track from a path or a dirt road so that the track starts a few metres into the forest or meadow, goes towards the road, crosses it, and continues on the other side of the road. Since you are only supposed to train one challenge at a time, you place the reward 20-30 metres after crossing the road. In this case it is often necessary that a person knowing where the track has been laid is present to watch the dog handler. Many dog handlers will mistrust the dog when she wants to pick up the track the wrong way. (Most tracks starting from or near a road tend to continue away from the road, not towards it).

It is equally possible to make this track longer if you wish. To do this you place a smaller reward in the first spot (20-30 metres after the road), with the real jackpot being at the end of the track. Do not forget the importance of placing the first reinforcement, as finding a treat after 700 metres is not a reward for the crossing of the road, but for the long track!

Rover in the dark

On a workshop in Sauerland, Germany, I met a dog that had lost his vision in a dramatic accident. He was totally blind, used his owner as a "guide human". He was very unsure, and moved hesitantly and unwillingly on unfamiliar ground. The first track we laid for him was roughly 8 metres long, made with short, shuffling steps and plenty of treats at the end. He sniffed the track but was anxious to move forward in the unknown darkness. Consequently, he ended up spinning a lot around his own nose without advancing along the track. The owner encouraged him and helped him forward until he reached the goal and received his very well deserved treat: a huge portion of chicken. This track had made him very tired, even though he had received a lot of support.

Many hours later we laid a new similar track for him. This time it was slightly shorter and with a tiny treat about every metre. He moved very hesitantly still, and still needed some help from his mum. But there was a tiny sign of progress. The following day, he was set a new track of about 5-6 metres with chicken pieces every metre. This time, slowly but surely, he followed the track without any help, safely finding the bowl containing his reward. For Rover, this was the beginning of trusting himself and his own senses without being dependent on walking as he was used to, supported by a tight lead or his nose touching the back of his owner's knee.

Chapter 12

Scent
Discrimination

How can you train your own dog to detect gluten, soya or traces of peanut in your food, a certain type of mushroom such as Chanterelles in the woods or explosives at an airport? In this chapter, I am using peanut oil as the example. You can equally well copy this training plan and use instead your own keys, Chanterelles, explosives, drugs, carrots, or whatever you choose. All you have to do is to acquire some of the exact substance that you are intending the dog to learn to search for. Pure gluten can be purchased in health shops, oils in food shops and pharmacies. Should you wish to train for Chanterelles, you will eventually have to go and find them growing in the woods.

Before starting your training you will need to do two things: firstly, decide what your dog should learn to find, and secondly research how to wash the item's scent away leaving no trace (choose perfume free soaps!) Only then are you ready to go further.

What is "scent discrimination"?
Quite simply, it is to discriminate between smells, or to pick one scent among others. A drugs dog, for example, can recognise the smell of a certain drug amongst the scents of food, sweat, leather, oil, tobacco: practically anything, in fact.

Obedience competitions have a test where the dog must find a little piece of cloth (or another item) that smells of the owner. The object is placed amongst other identical objects that do not smell of the owner. A dog's nose is easily capable of this.

On the borders of South Africa, for example, dogs are trained to recognise explosives, narcotics, rhino horn, rhino horn juice and ivory.

In nature, it is easy to recognise that the dog (or wolf!) is quite capable of smelling the difference between the track of a moose, hare, fox or another dog or wolf. And, depending on the dog's motivation, she will pick one of the tracks. The hungry and lone dog will probably follow the hare; the hungry dog with the support of the pack may pick the moose track. The full and lonely dog may choose the dog track. And, eventually, the full, contented dog may choose to do absolutely nothing.

Your dog's marking/reporting behaviour
Once your dog has found Chanterelles in the forest, explosives in a suitcase or peanut oil in the food, it will not help you unless the dog has a way of communicating with you. The dog must

have the means of reporting back to you or marking the find so that you will understand what was found and where. The marking behaviour may be many things, depending on what the dog is searching for and in which surroundings. Police dogs finding refugees will normally bark. Civilian dogs searching for lost persons will often mark by retrieving a special marker attached to their own collar. Dogs finding people in a ruin can mark by scratching the ground and/or barking. Land mines are marked by the dog sitting or laying motionless next to the mine.

To mark a find of Chanterelles, your dog can sit, bark or come back to fetch you, for instance.

No matter what you choose, this particular behaviour must be trained in advance. Your dog will need to develop a behaviour that can be reliably and happily offered, such as a bark, a sit, a down, a retrieve, a play bow or whatever. The task should be trained with exclusively positive associations, not by using punishment or any aversives. Scent discrimination, retrieve, or any exercise in fact that is trained by force is absolutely useless. My experience is that a behaviour which is shaped is a happy choice.

Another very good option is to just wait and see what your dog offers by herself!

A little practical advice

You may have foreseen a problem in training with peanut oil: it floats and cannot be laid anywhere. I use clean tin cans or jam jars. Paper or plastic cups may also be used, as long as you throw them away when they are contaminated by any oil.

I drip 2-3 drops of oil into my chosen container. Narrow cans (with no sharp edges) may be handy as many dogs will try to eat the oil. The containers should be identical both in size and colour in order to prevent the dog from solving the problem by looking at the container. Mark the containers to avoid mixing them up or contaminating other containers with peanut oil. Labels are also a good idea. Bear in mind that the labels and the pen will allow scent to evaporate (and the dog will be able to see it too), so you must have labels and markings on all the containers you use. If you are not sure whether you have spilt some peanut oil on any of the other containers, clean them all and start from the beginning.

Kwanza, a mine detection dog in Angola, has found traces of explosives. She is trained to report this by offering a sit. Instead, she stands still displaying a long series of calming signals: yawning, looking away, turning away, freezing, blinking, lifting a paw. Why should this be?

The reason is this: she is calming herself as a result of her old negative associations. But she does not leave either. Why not? Well, she does know she will get a reward for finding a mine, which she probably wants. On the other hand, she does not wish to sit because sit was originally trained by force: jerking the choke chain at the same time as she was pushed down by a hand on her hip. She has been working for 2-3 years, and now this negative association pops up like oil bubbling up from deep underground that will one day break through to the open air.

The solution? We took her out of operational work, and retrained her sit with positive associations. The cue had to be changed as well. After a couple of weeks, she was back in operation, this time willingly performing her task. How long for, I don't know however, as I left the project 8-10 months later. It is possible that the problem may recur later. At least the dog handler now knows how to cope with it.

Cleanliness and order are important key words.

Ok, we have established some tools, and now...

...the training may commence!

Scent discrimination is a discipline comprising several smaller parts: one part is the willingness to search, another is offering a marking behaviour and a further one is the knowledge of what to search for. In many cases a particular search pattern will be advisable.

So: the dog must know what to find, where to search, and how to communicate the find to you. And, of course, the dog must also have the desire to work for you.

Step by step training

First of all, you should decide upon which behaviour you would like the dog to show to indicate to you that the correct scent has been found. This is the marking behaviour, and may be a sit, a down or a bark for example. It may be that you have decided to let the dog choose the marking behaviour. Whichever choice you have made, I will assume that the training of this is already in place.

To keep a track on the progress of the training, it is useful to divide the aim into smaller, achievable and measurable steps. You should progress from one step to the next when your dog offers the correct behaviour 80% of the time, or 4 out of the 5 times she performs. If the dog is only getting 2 attempts correct out of 5 tries, take a step or two backwards. Never fail to keep to series of 1-5 repetitions between each break. You may be able to train several times per day, as long as you are careful to work in short sessions and give proper breaks.

Steps for peanut oil
(or chanterelle etc) training

1. associate something positive to the peanut oil

2. marking behaviour

3. add a "negative" scent

4. add two negative scents

5. gradually increase the number of negative scents, until the desired number or length is achieved

6. give the dog the chance to do a "negative search", i.e. search runs where there is no peanut oil. This serves to confirm her understanding that it is only peanut oil that should be found, and also helps to reassure the dog that there is nothing wrong when there is no peanut oil.

7. endurance, gradually increase the number of searches in a row

8. generalisation, i.e. train in various environments. Try to simulate (or go to!) such environments where the dog is supposed to work later.

9. put the behaviour on a cue

10. get a helper, so you can train unknown tasks

Step 1

The aim is to establish a positive association to peanut oil for your dog. Hold a container with peanut oil in front of the dog, and praise immediately the dog sniffs at it. Gradually hold the container further away, so that the dog has to take some initiative to be able to sniff the oil. You can, for example, leave the container on the ground, letting the dog take a few steps towards it.

Repeat this until the dog approaches the oil by herself to get her reward.

Step 2

The aim is to get the dog to report, or mark her find.

Ideally the scent of peanut oil should become the cue for marking.

Present the peanut oil to the dog. Whilst the dog sniffs it, delay half a second before your praise, and give the cue for the marking behaviour (bark or sit etc.) required. Reward even if the dog does not display the marking behaviour. Be aware that there is a lot on your dog's mind at this point! After 3-5 times the dog will normally start to perform on your cue.

A short cut to obtaining the marking behaviour required can be to warm up by training the marking behaviour immediately before the search work starts. With your enthusiasm for the chosen behaviour fresh in her mind, the dog will tend to offer this particular behaviour to please you again and thus make you supply more treats!

Repeat this until the dog marks spontaneously when she sniffs the peanut oil.

Marking a "find" with a sit

Step 3

At this stage the aim is to teach the dog that only peanut oil is the right choice, and that anything else is to be ignored.

Present your dog with the peanut oil in one container, and another oil, such as sunflower, in a second container. Arrange the two containers so that the peanut oil is in the container closest to the dog. Praise for sniffing the peanut oil. The first 3-4 times don't insist that the dog gives a marking behaviour even if she is able to. Ignore any sniffing at the wrong ("negative") oil. Whatever you do, keep yourself from saying "no" or "wrong" or "different" to the dog. If the dog won't leave the wrong oil, get an assistant to hold the containers and hide the wrong container behind his back. As soon as the dog sniffs the right oil, give her the jackpot!

Repeat this until the dog sits spontaneously by the peanut oil (or marks in any other appropriate way), and ignores the sunflower oil.

Step 4

The aim here is to increase the dog's self-confidence in choosing the correct oil.

The task now includes three containers, one of which contains peanut oil and the two other containers of different oils. Once again you ignore any interest in the "wrong" oils, and praise (maybe jackpot!) when the dog goes to the right one.

NB: you should interchange the position of the containers for each try the dog has at them: she is more clever than you know!

Repeat until the dog easily leaves the two wrong oils and picks the peanut oil, including correct marking behaviour.

Step 5

The aim is for the dog to search six containers and choose the correct oil.

Gradually increase the number of containers, as described in Step 4. Most systems where dogs are working in this way have 6-8 stations for the dogs to check. The containers may be in a row, a group or a circle: find out which layout best suits you and your dog.

Repeat until the dog easily and happily picks out the one positive oil from all 6 containers (or 8 if you prefer).

Step 6

This time the aim is for the dog to complete a search where no peanut oil is present and without making any false markings, instead reporting to you, "There is nothing here!".

To begin with, present the dog only one or two containers with alternative oils, and praise when the dog leaves the last container! Gradually increase the number of containers to 6 or 8. Ignore any false markings, reducing instead the number of containers to make it easier for the dog. This is the stage where timing of your praise may be critical. Only praise immediately after the dog has left the containers. Little by little delay your praise further, until the dog comes all the way back to you when no peanut oil is present.

Don't present the dog with too many negatives in a row. In between 1-3 negative runs, it is essential for the dog to search and find the real thing.

Repeat until the dog makes no mistakes!

Step 7

Now the aim is to work at establishing the dog's level of endurance.

You should decide how long you want your dog to work before a break is given. Do not demand too much, and only very slowly should you increase the duration for which the dog is expected to work. Do it so that it is not simply a gradual increase, but ensure that some working periods are shorter as well. It must not appear to become increasingly difficult for the dog! Be aware that every dog will have a different threshold here.

Repeat until you have found an appropriate duration for a search period.

Step 8

Here you should aim to generalise the search work.

You probably started the training in a peaceful place with few distractions. Now is the time to remember that your dog must be able to search in other areas and with other people, sounds and other distractions present. Imagine a real life situation: it may be necessary to search for peanut oil in your food in restaurants as well as in food stores. Strive for a gradual approach to such environments; perhaps if you are persuasive enough you may be able to arrange something with the owner of a restaurant or the manager of

Groenendal sniffs oil in a tin can

a supermarket, although this in itself will be an uphill struggle in some countries! When your dog is comfortable about working in one environment, change to a new one.

Repeat until your dog works undisturbed in the environments that are relevant to you.

Step 9

The aim is that the dog will start working on a given cue.

You may add the cue at an earlier stage, but you must never add the cue unless you know for certain that the dog will perform satisfactorily. My little test for whether to add the cue or not is to prepare a training session, and when the dog performs three times in a row I give the cue the fourth time. I really want to avoid the situation where I give the cue and the dog does not respond to it. For example, every time I call "come" and the dog does not come, the meaning of the cue loses value. This is the reason I am so careful about this. Give the cue in a well known environment the first few times, and go through step 8 the way I described previously: the first three times without the cue, then the fourth time with the cue in each new environment.

Repeat until the dog always responds satisfactorily to this cue. Good luck!

Eagerness!

Step 10

The aim is for you to trust your dog.

You need one or more helpers to prepare new and unknown tasks for you. The weakness so far, as you may have noticed, has of course been that you have always known the correct answer!

When it comes to reality, you will never know the answer, and of course that is why we started to train dogs for this in the first place.

The difficulty might be that you may have (unconsciously) established one way or another to show your dog where the positive sample is, either by slowing down, drawing or holding your breath or fiddling with the lead for example.

Repeat until your helper(s) confirm that you have learnt to trust your dog!

Further on down the road

Even though you have completed this programme successfully, you are only at the beginning of the work involved to get a fully trained peanut oil dog. Peanut oil occurs in food in various forms and concentrations. Further training will be necessary to take the dog through these same steps, using food that contains peanut oil, and food that is guaranteed to be free of it. One day, for example, you should work on pastry containing peanut oil and other oils, another day

on pastry that is baked on plates greased with the same variety of oils, etc. Work out all the different ways in which the oil may be presented: boiled, fried, cooled, fresh... also bear in mind that meat or fish fried in oil may be irresistible temptations for your dog! To keep up the motivation for the search work, the reward must be as good as or better than that which the dog is supposed to search for and leave without eating...

It goes without saying that you are never allowed to yell at or punish your dog for any mistakes. Mistakes will only occur if your preparation has not been good enough.

Besides, you will never really know whether your dog is right or not in her marking, will you?

Some final advice

The most common trap to fall into is to give attention to the dog when she is sniffing the wrong or negative oils. Any attention, positive or negative, is likely to be interpreted by your dog as a reward, and you may end up teaching your dog to mark falsely. Ways in which you might inadvertently give attention include pulling at the lead, saying "no", or laughing or sighing, for example. Instead of giving a negative reaction to any wrong behaviour, you must eliminate the chances of the dog getting any possible benefit out of doing the wrong thing. For example when the dog pays attention to the wrong oil, let the helper remove the can with this oil so the dog has no opportunity to get it wrong.

With dogs working independently like this, you need a dog that is very self confident.

During my work in both Angola and South-Africa I saw several good mine detection dogs being severely set back or even completely ruined, by being punished for false markings.

Accurate timing of your praise will be vital for what the dog learns. If you praise for approaching an object, the dog's interest in this object will increase. But if you praise when the dog is about to leave it, the dog will learn to leave the object alone. Watch your dog carefully!

I strongly suggest that you keep a training diary. I do not know how many times my pupils and I have discovered how stereotyped our training actually is until the day we start taking exact notes about what we do. We may think that we do it differently, but we tend to act in the same old patterns!

Many have also discovered that the same problems often occur at the same time of the year, and this too was not previously clear until they started to write their diary.

Chapter 13
Retrieve

Any dog can learn how to retrieve...

But is it ever necessary? Is it worth all the effort if you have a dog that really does not like to retrieve?

Even though the methods I describe are exclusively pleasant, I strongly suggest that you consider how important it is for you that your dog retrieves before you begin the training. In many instances it may be just as much fun and convenient to do the tricks and games using something edible instead.

If you still wish to teach your dog to carry things in her mouth, it is absolutely vital that you avoid any method that might include the least hint of pain, force or any other unpleasant experience for your dog, however mild.

The dog must learn that it is pleasant (and voluntary) to cooperate with you!

During the retrieve training, as with all other training, it is crucial that you never say "NO", even if the dog does something you regard as wrong. You never know with what your dog will associate your aggression. Your dog may believe you are annoyed because of your reaction if she

bites or approaches the object and this may result in her becoming afraid of retrieving. If you are really unlucky, the dog may become afraid of you as a direct result of your anger. It is far better to create a calm and friendly atmosphere for the training.

If you are lucky, there will be something in or around the house that your dog will put her teeth on voluntarily. Whatever this is, (acceptable or forbidden!), as long as it is safe this object will be the best starting point for the training. Get this object and hold it in front of your dog. As soon as your dog uses her teeth on it, praise and exchange with a treat.

If your dog doesn't want to put her teeth around the object whilst you hold it, place it on the ground in front of her. Praise and exchange with a treat whenever she puts her teeth on it. The treat must be good enough for the dog to let go of the object to grab the treat instead.

During this stage, you should aim to place your hand so that the object is dropped into it rather than on the floor. When your dog easily and willingly puts her teeth on or around the object and even offers it to you in exchange for a treat, it is time to place the object further away. But do not throw it yet. Your dog must walk a few steps to fetch the object, and carry it a few steps back to you. Great! Praise her and give a nice treat.

The next step could be to throw the object. Ensure that you always increase the difficulty for the dog, not too slowly and not too quickly. If your dog starts to play with or chew the object, start again calmly, placing the object in front of the dog. Always exchange the object with a treat before your dog starts to chew or play with it. This is your responsibility, not the dog's.

Increase the distance gradually. Again be careful not to increase the distance too quickly, and not to train for too long a session at a time.

If you train for too long, your dog may become fed up with the task, or may become too excited which may lead to making mistakes. By increasing the distance too fast, you risk your dog getting too excited, consequently being more likely to chew and play with the object instead of coming to you with it. You may very well play with the object, but only after your dog has given it to you.

If you find that there is absolutely nothing that your dog will lift with her mouth, think again.

What about food?

Try filling a sock with some very tasty treats, and knot it at the end. Lay the sock in front of your dog. As the dog bites at the sock praise and exchange with exactly the same treat, which you will of course have plenty of in your pocket. Or open the sock and give your dog some treats out of it. Do expect one or two socks to be destroyed, however! Remember that this will not be the dog's fault, but your own as it will mean that you have been too late in exchanging the sock for the treat. It may be that treat you are offering is of an inappropriate size or quality. In the eyes of the dog, whatever she "buys" from you must be of higher or equal value to the object given up. Dogs are good at making judgements such as these!

Repeat a few times, then take a break. Stop too early rather than too late.

After training a little, test to see if your dog will pick up a sock even when there is no food in it. Use the same sock initially, as it smells of food. If your dog picks it up, give a jackpot and show your dog that you are pleased. If she does not pick the sock up, put some food in it again, and continue as described. Gradually reduce the quantity of food in the sock, ensuring that nice treats are always available to buy from you in exchange for the sock.

Show your dog that there is a real purpose in picking up an empty sock as well!

When an empty sock works, try one without treats. When this one works, use something else.

Gradually increase the difficulty of the type of object your dog is required to pick up. Eventually, you may reach your goal: that your dog happily will pick up almost anything for you.

Hopefully, you will pretty quickly reach the stage where you can now leave behind the one and only object that your dog was previously interested in and instead train your dog to retrieve other types of things. When you have warmed up 2-3 times retrieving something easy, all of a sudden drop a new object on the ground. If your dog picks it up or maybe only puts her teeth around it, praise and give a jackpot.

Make it easy for you and your dog: always start with things that your dog finds nice to put her mouth around. Doing a little research will help you find out what your dog prefers, but always ensure the dog's safety. Some dogs love plush toys, others fall for leather toys. Rubber toys or wooden items are great for other dogs. Gloves, the kids' toys, anything that is not harmful may be used. Over time, you can train your dog to lift up all kinds of things: forks, coffee mugs, little coins, corks from bottles, relatively heavy metal objects, buckets, the long handled scrubbing brush, things that rattle or make other sounds. Just let your imagination run riot, and this will be a game of great fun for you both.

A third possibility to train a dog to retrieve is to follow the steps described in chapter 8, stage 2. This method is based upon shaping. Follow the steps from the very beginning, but rather than being satisfied with pawing or something else, carry on until your dog puts her teeth on or bites at the object.

Here is a short repetition of the steps, including what to praise and treat for:

The dog:

1. looks at the object
2. sniffs the object
3. takes a step towards the object
4. licks it
5. bites at it
6. holds it, maybe for a second or two

After this, it is your challenge to manipulate things so that the object finds its way into your hand, and for the dog to then carry it for an increasingly greater length of time, as described in the sock-paragraph above.

No matter which method you choose initially, continue to work in the same way: only when your dog is able to carry the object several steps, should you throw it for her. Until now, you should have always placed it on the ground.

Throwing the object may be too intense or exciting for many dogs, with the whole episode resulting in more running and chewing than real training.

It may be wise to put the retrieve behaviour on cue. Some dogs love to retrieve items to gain attention, and you can avoid this by teaching the dog that the only time you want something brought to you is when you have asked for it. Therefore, ensure that you only ever praise and pay your dog for retrieving once you have given a cue.

My suggestion always focuses on the dog giving up the object to the hand whilst being in front of you. If you wish to encourage any other form of delivery, or if you want to go to competitions or meet some special demands, it is wise to start training for these specifics at this point.

The most important thing above all is that *both* you and the dog have fun together.

The Kingdom of Scent
Bibliography

Sources and references

Rugaas, Turid: On Talking Terms with Dogs: Calming Signals. Sheila Harper Ltd (Qanuk Ltd) 2005   ISBN 0-954 8032-1-3 (see overleaf for further details)

Pryor, Karen: Don't Shoot the Dog: The New Art of Teaching and Training. Bantam Books 2002   ISBN 0-553-38039-7

Pryor, Karen: Lads Before the Wind. Washington: Sunshine Books 1994   ISBN 1-8909-4804-7

Järverud, Svend og Järverud Gunvor af Klinteberg: Din Hund praktisk hundebok. Wennergren-Cappelen AS 1986

Järverud, Svend og Järverud Gunvor af Klinteberg (1986) Din Hund fortsätter Beteende – inlärning – moment. Solna: Naturia Förlag 1986

Standard Operating Procedures Manual for Mechem Explosive & Drug Detection System Vol I & Vol II. Mechem International Ltd., West Sussex England. (not available to the general public)

Kaldenbach, Jan: K9 Scent Detection My Favorite Judge lives in a Kennel. Alberta CAN: Detselig Enterprises Ltd. 1998

Hallgren, Anders &Hallgren, Marie Hansson: Kantarellsök med Hund. Vagnhärad: Jycke-Tryck AB 1990

Jones, Deborah A. Ph.D.: Click n Sniff: Clicker training for Scent Discrimination. Eliot ME: Howln Moon Press

Bru, Kristin Meitz & Kittelsen, Silje: "Fra lederskap til lederrolle", Canis nr 2/03

Bru, Kristin Meitz & Kittelsen, Silje: "Fra lederskap til lederrolle", foredrag ved NAS høstseminar, Oslo November 2002.

Visit our website shop **www.sheilaharper.co.uk**
for an extensive range of books, DVDs, equipment and accessories.

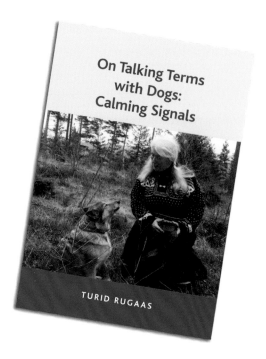

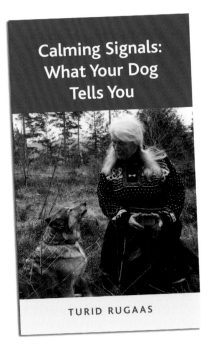

Turid Rugaas:
On Talking Terms with Dogs:
Calming Signals

Turid Rugaas' revolutionary work incorporates what is probably the single most important study of canine social language. Turid has been observing and analysing calming signals for years; she has documented over 30 signals and presents her findings in this book along with photographic illustrations and explanations of why and how they are used. By studying these signals and improving our powers of observations we can increase our ability to communicate with our dogs.

If you have ever wondered what your dog is trying to tell you then this is the book for you!

Revised/updated with new material and colour photographs

Published 2005 82 pages. ISBN: 0-954 8032-1-3

Companion Video and DVD -
Calming Signals:
What Your Dog Tells You
by Turid Rugaas

The companion to Turid's best selling book: On Talking Terms With Dogs is available on both video and DVD. Turid presents us with a unique opportunity to see footage of dogs using calming signals, increasing our own ability to study and observe the signals. Turid, who is the foremost authority in the world on dog language, gives explanations and shows us how we can use calming signals in our own interactions with dogs. Become an addictive dog-watcher with this fascinating, compulsive viewing.

Now you too can truly be "on talking terms with dogs"!

Viewing time approximately 45 minutes. Video in PAL format for British/European VCR's.

DVD languages: English, German and French

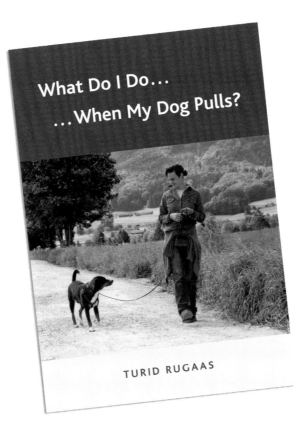

Turid Rugaas –
What Do I Do When My Dog Pulls?

Norwegian dog trainer Turid Rugaas, best known for her ground-breaking work on calming signals, describes her kind and effective method for encouraging dogs to walk without pulling.

Quick and easy to learn, the method can be applied to any dog no matter what size, breed or age. Dogs that are easily distracted, or that encounter situations where they may lunge, bark or give aggressive displays can be helped to walk calmly and quietly on a slack leash. City, town or country walking can all become more relaxed, reducing stress for dog and owner.

Turid's method is explained in simple steps with informative photographs which aid understanding, and the book includes tips on equipment to use, reasons for pulling and trouble shooting, along with case studies.

Published 2004 64 pages. ISBN 0-954 8032-0-5

Courses by Sheila Harper

Sheila Harper Ltd offers a wide range of canine behaviour and training courses throughout the UK. Practical and theoretical courses for pet owners or professionals, ranging from nosework and games to communication, body language and understanding dogs. Course topics vary annually.

For further information visit our website: www.sheilaharper.co.uk

Essential Oils

Games for Dogs

Activity Holidays

Handling Skills

Nutrition

Rescue & Re-homing

Retrieve

Instructing Classes

Canine Communication